Purposeful Play

KRISTINE MRAZ

ALISON PORCELLI

CHERYL TYLER

Purposeful Play

A Teacher's Guide to Igniting Deep and Joyful Learning Across the Day

HEINEMANN
Portsmouth, NH

Heinemann
361 Hanover Street
Portsmouth, NH 03801–3912
www.heinemann.com

Offices and agents throughout the world

Cataloging-in-Publication data is on file at the Library of Congress
ISBN: 978-0-325-07788-8

Editors: Zoë Ryder White and Katie Wood Ray
Production Editor: Patty Adams
Cover and Interior Design: Monica Ann Crigler
Cover and Interior Photographer: Jesse Angelo
Typesetter: Kim Arney
Manufacturing: Steve Bernier

Printed in the United States of America on acid-free paper
20   19   18   VP   5

To my sister, Jen, for the endless hours we played together,
and my partner Geoff, the funniest person I know
—Kristi Mraz

To my husband, Tom, and my son, Preston, who both bring joy
and a spirit of playfulness into my life everyday
—Alison Porcelli

To the staff and volunteers at Animal Haven who bring play
into the lives of neglected and abused cats and dogs
—Cheryl Tyler

CONTENTS

ACKNOWLEDGMENTS

We'd like to thank . . .

Our editors, Zoë Ryder White and Katie Wood Ray who believed in our project from the very beginning and cheered us on every step of the way. Thank you for your insightful advice and steadfast encouragement. We'd also like to thank the in-house team at Heinemann, particularly Patty Adams, Eric Chalek, Monica Crigler, and Pam Hunt, for making our book beautiful and for supporting our vision along the way.

Our profound respect and thanks to Adele Schroeter, principal of PS 59 in Manhattan, for being the kind of leader who puts kids first and always makes sure there is time for play. Thank you for pushing us to be better for our children and for allowing us to use PS 59 as our playground for this work.

Thank you to all of the teachers at PS 59. We feel fortunate to be a part of such an inspiring community of professionals who have the utmost respect for kids and teach us to outgrow ourselves each and every day.

We feel fortunate to have worked with a number of teachers who have created joyful and playful classrooms, particularly Cara Biggane, Rebecca Ravski, Kathryn Cazes, Jung Choe, Jennifer Frish, Michelle Hernandez, Lizzie Kimmel, Katie Lee, Joe Weaver, and Nekia Wise. Thank you for opening your doors and for going along on this "joy" ride with us.

We each have a very special connection to the Teachers College Reading and Writing Project—where we all met—and are grateful to all of our colleagues there for helping to shape our beliefs about teaching and learning and for inspiring kids and teachers across the world. In particular, we thank Lucy Calkins, whose extraordinary vision and leadership makes so much possible; Kathleen Tolan, who embodies the meaning of passion; Laurie Pessah, who buoyed us; Shanna Schwartz for her generosity of spirit, and Amanda Hartman, whose vision of social justice and equity inspires us.

We thank Jennifer Serravallo, who always believed in this work and who encouraged us to write the book for Lola, Vivian, and all kids. We also thank Kathy Collins for her humor, joy, and the play she infuses in every interaction.

Our deepest gratitude to our photographer, Jesse Angelo, for capturing children being children across the beautiful pages of this book and for infusing it with energy and joy.

Thanks to Marjorie Martinelli for being a devoted friend and colleague, one who's willing to labor through a bibliography. Thank you for your diligence, timeliness, and attention to detail.

Alison would first like to thank her coauthors, Kristi and Cheryl, two of the most brilliant kindergarten teachers she has ever met. She is honored to have written this book with you. To all of Alison's former kindergarten students from Guilderland and Armonk, NY, who taught her the importance of making time for play each day. To Alison's dear friends and primary colleagues from her time at the Teachers College Reading and Writing Project, particularly Dahlia Dallal, Christine Holley, Monique Knight, Jory Lieber, Beth Moore, Marika Paez Wiesen, and Sarah Picard Taylor, who taught her so much about collaboration, hard work, and joyful teaching. Alison thanks her family for encouraging and inspiring endless hours of play while growing up, from putting on shows and building forts to doing "the coffee break." Finally, she would like to thank her husband, Tom—thank you for your constant love and support and for being the kind of father who encourages playfulness and curiosity. And to her son, Preston, the best gift life has given her. You are a joy to watch at play.

Cheryl would like to thank her co-authors, Alison and Kristi. She is in awe of their wisdom, insight, humor, and passion for creating schools where kids are able to imagine unlimited possibilities. She would like to thank the wise teachers of PS 277 in the South Bronx who used the inquiry rooms to pave the way and infused the joy of play throughout the day: Adele Cammarata, Laura Zatkowsky, Tiana Silvas, Stacy Schellhaas, Ruairi Gribbon, Ali Siotkas, Robyn Levy, Joe Weaver, Jenna Campbell, William Seward, Danielle Feuer, Cara Biggane, Michelle Hernandez, Rebecca Ravski, Jessica Stillman, Nickie Coleman, Laura Heisler Cogan, Marcia Reidy, Kristin Smith, Mike Ochs, Lauren Perovich, Caitlin Mahoney, and Denise Capasso. Cheryl's deepest thanks go to her colleagues and partners in learning at Teachers College Reading and Writing Project, in particular, Beth Neville for her wisdom and sage advice, Julia Mooney, an extraordinary writer and friend, Angela Baez, Lindsay Barton, Ryan Candelario, Rebecca Cronin, Celena Larkey, Lindsay Mann, Rachel Rothman, and Katie Wears for their passion for play and wise counsel. And then there are those friends who just make life interesting, joyful, and playful: thanks to Jacqui Getz for her fearlessness and humor, Susan Felder for her steadfastness, Lucy Malka for her limitless wisdom, Joe Yukish, who lives a life of purpose and play, and Dylan, the wisest, kindest friend a mom could ask for.

Kristi would like to thank her coauthors, Cheryl and Alison, for being a source of thoughtful conversation, reflective questioning, and constant laughter. She could not have asked for a better and more joyful collaboration. She would also like to thank the families and children she has worked with the past few years who have taught her there is no greater learning than that which happens through play. Friends and teachers like Valerie Geschwind and Christine Hertz provided brilliance and sanity checks throughout the entire process. Chris Lehman, Kristin Ziemke, Kate Roberts, and Maggie Beattie Roberts inspire with their very being, and Kristi would like to thank them for every laugh, every talk, and their way of being fully and joyfully in the world. Finally, she would like to thank her family. First, to her sister, who endured hours of playing Little House on the Prairie in a dark and musty basement, and to her husband, Geoff, a talented writer and comedian, who has never failed to make her laugh.

Purposeful Play

Play is joy and play is work.

Section 1

All About Play

*The Reasons,
Research,
and Resources*

PLAY ISN'T A LUXURY.
IT'S A NECESSITY.

It is kindergarten in November, and there is a hum in the classroom generated by four- and five-year-olds deeply immersed in imaginary play. Only recently have some of these children moved from contentedly building individual projects side by side to creating imaginary play worlds collaboratively with their peers. Some children are constructing the Empire State Building out of Magna-Tiles (Figure 1.1), while other children have been building and rebuilding a zombie haunted house inspired by a Halloween book. Over in the sand table, an ice cream stand has opened, and in a group of large cardboard boxes, a family theme is emerging, or trying to at least.

An argument brewing between two girls has gathered a small crowd of onlookers.

"I said, 'I am the mommy!'" Julia yells, fists balled, feet stamping.

"But you are always the mommy! I am the mommy now!" Maya retorts.

"I am the mommy all day, and then you can be the mommy a different day!" Julia decides.

"You are always the mommy. It's not fair! I'm not playing anymore," Maya screams.

Their teacher, Lauren, is watching from a distance, observing how these two girls are negotiating this problem, trying to decide if they need a little coaching, when suddenly their fellow student Sara enters the fray.

"Why don't you have two mommies?" she suggests.

The two girls stare at her, until Julia asserts, "You can only have one mommy. And one daddy."

Sara says, "I have two mommies."

Lauren watches as Julia and Maya try to assimilate this information into their existing family schema, wondering what this new knowledge will prompt in their play.

Julia is unbudging. "There is only one mommy. I'm the mommy." She turns abruptly and begins washing dishes. Maya sighs but then picks up the block the students have transformed into a smartphone and begins talking animatedly. Sara drifts back over to the haunted house she is building with several others.

Figure 1.1 Constructing the Empire State Building.

Lauren scribbles furiously on her clipboard. She sees room for these girls to grow in their ability to negotiate and problem solve and opportunities to teach more into the language of emotions. She also sees that there are good questions brewing about important kindergarten concepts, most obviously, "What makes a family?" Lauren decides that it might be time to launch a family inquiry, which is one of the social studies topics for her grade.

Lauren heads over to check in with Julia and Maya to see if the problem has resolved. It has in the way that many of these small conflicts do: with compromise. Maya has contented herself to be the older sister in college, while Julia is the mom. Lauren investigates a little further and finds that Maya has decided it is OK for her to wait to be the mommy until the next day. Julia agrees. Knowing the mercurial nature of five-year-olds, and also teaching into a planning strategy to avoid conflict, Lauren suggests they leave themselves a note at the end of choice time to remind themselves that they plan to swap roles tomorrow.

Later that same day, Lauren returns to the question that arose earlier in the family center. She knows she will need some time to gather materials and think through the steps of the inquiry, but she is eager to leverage the children's natural curiosities into big questions. She gathers the children together and tells the story of the argument, ending with, "and that got me thinking, maybe we could investigate: What is a family? Do you think we could do some big thinking work about that?"

Over the next few weeks, the children begin a deep study of families. They study pictures of families, read books, interview family members, and develop theories about what makes a family and what roles people in families might have. Lauren is careful to ensure the books she reads aloud and the video clips she selects include diverse elements that are not reflected in her student population. Slowly, an understanding begins to emerge: Families are the people who care for you and love you. As this understanding emerges in conversation, Lauren is also sensitive to its appearance in children's play. How tight are the definitions of roles in play? Does the mommy always take care of the baby while the daddy goes to work? Can there be more than one mommy or daddy? Can there be no mommy or daddy? Then one day, weeks after the study has started, Lauren sees an argument around roles begin in a center that has chosen to play family. It appears that every child wants to be either a mommy or a baby.

Keyanna steps into the center of the conversation and points to the two children who want to be the mom. "You can all be mommies." She then gestures to herself and two other children, "And we can all be babies. It doesn't matter as long as we all love each other." The children agree and go off to build the space for their home (Figure 1.2).

Figure 1.2 Problem resolved, the babies are waiting for their mommies to come home from work.

In this moment, children are demonstrating powerful learning. They are demonstrating what rigor can look like when it is redefined to mean big thinking in child-friendly ways. They are also, coincidentally, playing. There is an argument in the world that suggests that play can happen only when work is done, yet children show us time and time again that play is the way they work. This book argues that play is an essential pillar of school, and of childhood. This book will take you through research and theory, classroom practice and application, and ways to infuse play throughout the day, whether you are teaching kindergarten or third grade. Every educator is pushed and pulled to make decisions regarding how to best teach their children; so first, here are a few reasons why you might choose play.

Why Choose Play? Answers to Common Questions About the Role of Play

We Follow the Common Core State Standards. How Does Play Fit with Meeting the Many Standards?

The Common Core State Standards are an endpoint, not a curriculum. Imagine the standards as a destination, like a point on a map. Reaching that destination involves an endless array of choice. Do you walk, or do you drive? Do you take the scenic route or the highway? Do you want to have less traffic but more stop lights, or more traffic and no lights? Likewise, when it comes to the Common Core State Standards, no map dictates how you get there, just that you need to get there.

Play allows multiple opportunities and modes to reach various standards (Figure 1.3). The Common Core State Standards for Speaking and Listening state that children need to follow agreed-upon rules for conversations. Play is rife with opportunities for engaging in discussions with peers, which Maya and Julia do to sort out their disagreement over who can be the mommy. Making the note to remind themselves of who will be the mommy the next day meets the standard for language, which states that children should spell using phonics knowledge. Children at play can often be found re-enacting favorite stories, like those in the haunted house center, which meets the standard for reading fiction, which states that children should be able to retell texts with key details. Informed teachers can see the standards being met in authentic and joyful play and help design engaging instruction that helps children meet the rest. What we need to teach may not always be a choice, but how we teach can be. Play is its own method of instruction.

Figure 1.3 Play or an introduction to STEM principles? It depends on the stance of the teacher.

How Can There Be Time for Play When There Is Such an Emphasis on Academic Rigor?

Well, first we need to define what *academic rigor* actually means. According to Barbara Blackburn, author of *Rigor Is Not a Four-Letter Word*, "Rigor is creating an environment in which each student is expected to learn at high levels, each student is supported so he or she can learn at high levels, and each student demonstrates learning at high levels" (2013, 13). We believe that play is one type of environment where children can be rigorous in their learning. You might be thinking, "Huh? Rigorous play? Isn't that an oxymoron?" The truth is when four-, five-, six-, and seven-year-olds play, they are able to achieve things at the farthest edge of their zone of proximal development (Vygotsky, 1978). Think about the child who industriously creates a sign for the airport in blocks saying, "JetBlue" (Figure 1.4) while in writing workshop he only adds labels to his writing when prompted and supported by the teacher. Think about the English language learner in your classroom who surprises you when she carries on a conversation with her peers during choice time or at recess, while during academic times she seems to answer only yes or no questions and only when prompted. Play is a natural learning environment for children, and it is something they have been doing their whole lives before coming to school. Because play is safe and familiar, children feel free to take risks and try on new learning.

Academic rigor also means giving our students the skills necessary to be successful in the twenty-first-century workplace. According to Tony Wagner (2008), an essential skill needed in the twenty-first century is imagination. There is no better place to develop a child's imagination than in play. When children engage in imaginative play, not only do they develop their creativity, they learn to be flexible thinkers, and they develop core social skills, such as negotiation, collaboration, and empathy. If we look back at Maya and Julia's imaginative play scenario, we can see all of this in action. They are developing their flexibility and creativity when they pretend the block is a smartphone, and they are developing the

Figure 1.4 In play, children create their own rigor. This child made a sign for the JetBlue terminal at the airport.

skills of negotiation and collaboration when they come to a compromise about who gets to be the mommy. Talk is an inherent and essential aspect of play. We believe that all of the skills children learn during play contribute to and enhance academic rigor in the classroom.

Figure 1.5 These second graders discuss the play they plan to perform during snack.

But What About My Students Who Need Extra Support? Wouldn't Their Time Be Better Spent Engaged in Small-Group Instruction?

Small-group work is a powerful instructional method and an important intervention for students who need additional support. However, small-group instruction should not replace play. All students, particularly those with different learning needs, should spend time playing as well as engaging in small-group instruction (Figure 1.5). Jennifer Serravallo's book, *Teaching Reading in Small Groups* (2010), is a wonderful resource for how to differentiate and make the most of your small-group instruction.

Play gives access to content and higher levels of thinking for a variety of learners. For example, Maya had difficulty composing narratives during writing time but, as seen in the scenario above, could readily engage in pretend play with elaborate story lines. Why is that? When children have access to a rich play environment (Figure 1.6), they are given an opportunity to learn and express their thinking through multiple sign systems. Sign systems are different ways of communicating. Art, music, drama, and language are all

Figure 1.6 In the foreground a child paints, while in the background a group plays ninja training camp.

considered sign systems (Short, Harste, and Burke, 1996). When children engage in choice time—one type of play environment—they are given opportunities to build with blocks, paint on an easel, and dramatize stories.

Not all learners use language as their primary mode of learning and expression; some benefit from movement and physicality while learning, whereas others express themselves best through drawing or painting. Think of the movie, *Akeelah and the Bee*, where the main character of the film, Akeelah, finally was able to learn her spelling words when she simultaneously jumped rope and spelled out loud. Ultimately, choice time is a way of tapping into our students' strengths to give them access to learning at higher levels. Isn't that the quintessential form of differentiation?

How Much Time in the Day Do Children Really Need to Play? Can't Children Just Play When They Are Finished with Their Work?

Russian psychologist Lev Vygotsky was a proponent of the idea that children learn best when we build on their strengths, but accomplishing this can sometimes feel a bit frustrating. As we struggle mightily to develop kids' stamina to ten, fifteen, or twenty minutes of reading and writing, we watch these same children deeply engaged in play during recess and choice time for long, extended periods. So while we firmly believe in building on children's strengths, it can be frustrating when we find ourselves limiting the time we give kids to do what we know they do best: play.

Figure 1.7 A teacher supports a child at work.

Perhaps, we need to look at play from a different perspective; if the feeling of active movement toward a goal is what we call work, then play *is* the work of children (Figure 1.7). In fact, it is the work and the art of childhood: the essence of learning, discovery, and creating. In play, learners are developing ideas, taking on and assigning roles, collaborating, crafting the environment and deciding when to change it, developing and negotiating rules, and being active listeners. If play is the work of children, then to build on kids' strengths, we need to ask, "How can we infuse an abundance of play and the principles of play across the curriculum?"

When children are dramatizing a favorite book, they are engaged in high-level comprehension skills including inference, interpretation, and synthesis. Think about the abstract thinking that happened when Julia and Maya transformed a block into a smartphone, or the metaphorical thinking of five-year-olds when they line up hollow blocks to replicate the restroom in the Empire State Building. Or the empathetic stance first graders are taking when they decide that the troll in "The Three Billy Goats Gruff" is mean because his mom sends him to school with messy hair, and they build a barber shop so the troll can get his hair cut. The thinking that occurs in play fits a definition of work (active engagement toward achieving a goal) and often provides impetus to continue working long after the official "play" time is done.

Figure 1.8 Ample time to play means ample time to build literacy skills: a kindergarten sign for the "Pink Berry."

Figure 1.9 Ample time to play also means ample time to build math skills: A first grader counts out change at the "grocery store."

Isn't Play Just "Fun"?

In *A Child's Work: The Importance of Fantasy Play* (2005), Vivian Gussin Paley tells us that the first time she heard the idea that play is the work of children was in 1949 when she was taking an undergraduate course at Sophie Newcomb College in New Orleans. Her instructor, Rena Wilson, told her students, "You are watching the only age group in school that is always busy making up its own work assignments.

Figure 1.10 The building of this structure required planning, collaboration, trial and error, and flexibility—not to mention the beginnings of understandings about engineering.

Figure 1.11 These girls are not just playing store, they are building literacy skills (speaking, listening, and writing), math skills (paying and receiving change), learning social studies concepts, (needs and wants), and abstract thinking (a block as a sandwich). Play does it all!

It looks and sounds like play, yet we properly call this play the work of children. Why? That is what you are here to find out." Ms. Wilson asked her undergraduate students to pretend that they were children who were playing and to consider what they were trying to accomplish and what obstacles they met. She wanted her college students to recall what it was like to be a child.

Paley shares what she and her classmates discovered in the course of creating, collaborating on, negotiating, and determining rules for fantasy play, that play is a complex activity that is, indeed, hard work (Figures 1.10 and 1.11). And they also realized that play is the work that coalesces all other enterprise in the classroom. It is serious business; just think about Julia and Maya at play and the words of John Dewey come to mind, "No one has ever watched a child intent in his play without being made aware of the complete merging of playfulness and seriousness" (Cuffaro, 1995, 85).

In Stuart Brown's seminal book, *Play: How It Shapes the Brain, Opens the Imagination, and Invigorates the Soul* (2010), he argues that play has an essential role in fueling our happiness and intelligence throughout our lives and that it is as essential to our health as sleep and food. Great thinkers and philosophers including Aristotle, Plato, Rousseau, Freud, Piaget, Vygotsky, and Einstein have put forth their thinking that play is not a frivolity but essential for the development of the mind and human spirit. Play connects us to the world and to each other and offers unlimited possibilities. So come. Let's play!

BALANCED PLAY

How It Makes Kids' Lives Better

Try to think of the last time you played. For many of us, we roam about our minds trying to recall instances where we played with dolls, or toys, or with games, but play is much more broadly defined than we often realize. Play takes on a myriad of forms and is defined more by the mindset we achieve when engaged in it than the materials or actions involved in it. Play, in all of its forms, is an essential part of a healthy and happy life (Figure 2.1). Stuart Brown, author of *Play*, writes, "When someone doesn't keep an element of play in their life, their core being will not be light. Play gives us the irony to deal with paradox, ambiguity and fatalism" (2010, 202). In short, play is also what keeps us functioning well as humans. For children,

Figure 2.1 Play builds persistence and resilience.

play is the furnace in which much of their brain development is forged. In a review of many prominent research studies regarding play, *Play for a Change*, Stuart Lester and Wendy Russell write, "The emerging evidence from the brain sciences suggests that playing, as a spontaneous, flexible, and goalless 'as-if' behavior, plays a significant role in the development of the brain's structure and chemistry, which gives rise to emotional and physical health, well-being and resilience, as well as laying the foundations for cognitive functioning and social competence" (2008, 45).

So what is play exactly? How do we identify it? What forms can it take? Part of utilizing play effectively in a classroom is understanding its complexity. This chapter will take you through the key features of any kind of play, identify the most common forms play can take, and walk you through a progression of play that many children go through.

What Is Play?

The key to leveraging play into all aspects of the school day and life is understanding that, above all else, play is intensely personal. For Kristi, moving furniture is a playful, joyful activity; for her husband it is sheer agony. For Cheryl, play is walking shelter dogs, when for others, such an act would be considered a chore. For

Figure 2.2 Considering risk on the playground.

Alison's sixteen-month-old son, Preston, pulling all of the toilet paper off the roll is sheer play ecstasy; for his parents, not so much. The challenge in defining play is that almost anything can be play if it fulfills certain characteristics, and it is these characteristics that make play so essential for brain development.

The authors of *Play for a Change* define play as, "what children and young people do when they follow their own ideas, in their own way and for their own reasons" (2008, 10). More specifically, the authors list: personal choice, control, feelings of power, opportunities to be nonliteral (rearranging the world to match what a child wants), intrinsically motivated, and pleasurable feelings as being essential aspects of play (10). Stuart Brown, author of *Play*, names many of the same concepts, adding in "freedom from time" and "improvisational potential" (2010, 17). In short, something is play if you have chosen to do it, have the capacity to pretend and change as you go, and enjoy it for the most part. This does not mean, however, that play is always "nice" or "safe." In fact, "children deliberately seek out uncertainty (both physical and emotional) in their play" (Lester and Russell, 2008, 11). True play always involves a certain amount of safe risk (Figure 2.2), and through navigating that risk, children and adults learn ways to survive in the real world, both emotionally and physically.

Why Is Play Valuable?

The shocking thing about play is that it is not limited to just humans. Watch any animal and you will see it engage in play behaviors, but why? "[Play] has evolved over eons in many animal species to promote survival. It shapes the brain and makes animals smarter and more adaptable. In higher animals, it fosters empathy and makes possible complex social groups" (Brown, 2010, 5). So how does play benefit us? Each feature of play—uncertainty, opportunities for improvisation, creating alternate realities, and the inherent pleasure—work across a myriad of brain systems. "Play may be a way of shaping the brain, maintaining plasticity and potential, and developing a positive emotional orientation and disposition that will enable more complex and playful interaction with the environment" (Lester and Russell, 2008, 20). To us, this also sounds like a definition of the purpose of school: growing optimism, flexibility, resilience, and an ability to deal with complex situations.

According to Lester and Russell, play can help with the development of emotional regulation. "The design features of play—uncertainty, flexibility, and 'as-if' frames—enable children to develop repertoires for avoiding emotional overreaction through a range of play strategies such as courage, bravery, resilience, and sociability" (2008, 20). When Maya and Julia encounter a disagreement in Chapter 1, Maya regulates her own desires by agreeing to "be the mommy" on the next day. Maya's ability to compromise will have long-lasting benefits as a student and as a child.

Play also helps to develop an individual's stress-response system. "Play creates the opportunity to create and resolve uncertainty, not so much when placing oneself in jeopardy, but more in relation to feelings of excitement, courage and resilience in the face of imagined disaster" (Lester and Russell, 2008, 20). In a typical family-play theme, when the babies run away from their mommies, the children playing babies are testing out ideas of independence in a safe way, and the children playing mommies are confronting the stress of finding them while building confidence to face challenge in the real world.

Play develops creativity as well. "Play supports adaptive variability rather than logical and narrow responses" (Lester and Russell, 2008, 21). In the vignette that opens Chapter 1, when multiple children want to play the same role, Keyanna's flexibility and willingness to play creatively with the family structure means the playing can continue. Keyanna and her playmates are innovating and improvising, which is an essential skill when it comes to problem solving across domains.

To put this in a recess context, imagine a group of children playing superheroes on a playground. As they leap and do battle with a villain, deep in their brains they are developing courage and resilience. As they grab blocks to use as shields, they are employing creativity and adaptability, and when they revise their play to be more gentle after someone gets bumped too hard, they are developing emotional regulation (Figure 2.3). These budding skills are essential to schooling, and to life in general. As Lester and Russell write, "what play may do is help children to be better children, rather than help them prepare to be adults" (2008, 19).

There is often such a desire in schools to focus on what children need next that we forget what children need now. Play gives children exactly what they need now, which will help them develop into the kinds of people who can handle what comes next. This essential play falls into different categories, each with its own unique benefits for children and for schools. Much like balanced literacy instruction, we need to provide opportunities for balanced play. Each kind of play facilitates children with different aspects of social, emotional, or cognitive development. When all types of play are offered across the day, the benefits of play are strengthened. In balanced literacy, shared reading, read aloud, focus lessons, phonics,

Figure 2.3 In the absence of sports equipment, blocks become hockey sticks, and the game is on!

and independent reading work in concert in the teaching of reading. Similarly, there is reciprocity among fantasy play, constructive play, games with rules, and rough-and-tumble play that enhances children's development.

Kinds of Play

Fantasy/Imaginative Play

In fantasy play, children choose an imaginary scenario in which they take on and act out roles and then determine a set of rules from these roles. For example, when playing "grocery store," children take on clearly understood roles of cashier, shopper, and announcer, and their actions are determined by those roles (Figures 2.4 and 2.5). Self-regulation becomes essential as children develop and adhere to sets of rules that define those roles.

Sometimes, fantasy play and reality intersect in interesting ways. Lev Vygotsky (1966) wrote about two sisters, ages five and seven, who began to play "sisters." When playing "sisters," the girls would dress alike, hold hands, and tell people how similar they were. In other words, they followed the perceived rules of how sisters might be expected to act. In reality, their sisterhood was much different. Sometimes they played together, sometimes they fought, and often they had nothing to do with each other. There was a greater degree of self-regulation and the following of rules when the girls were playing "sisters."

Because fantasy play often requires the substitution of one object for another, it also

Figure 2.4 Free samples at the grocery store.

Figure 2.5 Everyone has a role at the grocery store.

Figure 2.6 These kindergarten students have created an ice cream store with blocks, paper, and odds and ends from the classroom.

develops abstract thinking. When playing "restaurant," a hollow block can serve as a large pot for making soup, while other hollow blocks become the tables and chairs for the customers. As children begin to think abstractly, they conceptualize or generalize their understanding that a single object can have multiple meanings. This kind of abstract thinking is an essential tool for higher-level thinking and is often mandated in state standards, including the Common Core.

For more on how fantasy play develops, see Appendix A.

Constructive Play

Constructive play is an organized form of play that is, in many ways, goal- and product-oriented. Children use materials to create something, an activity that increases in complexity as they get older. Most constructive play happens in classrooms during choice time and typically involves playing or constructing with three-dimensional materials like blocks, playdough, art materials, and recycled materials (Figures 2.6 and 2.7).

Figure 2.7 Constructing with Legos.

Storytelling and dramatic reenactments of stories incorporate constructive play. In *A Quick Guide to Boosting English Acquisition in Choice Time*, Porcelli and Tyler talk about Story Play, where children reenact and represent the stories that they've been reading and writing. Using fabric to create costumes and hollow blocks and mural paper to build settings, "Readers step into the shoes of a character and writers envision in such a way that they write with vividness and power" (2008, 58). This sort of constructive play with stories is essential because the thinking children do when they're engaged in it actually deepens their connections to the literacy curriculum in many ways.

Because of its enormous potential for problem solving, connecting, deepening understanding, and replicating learning with open-ended materials, constructive play is one way to keep math, science, and engineering relevant in our classrooms (Figure 2.8).

As children examine, explore, sort, and arrange materials, ideas and imagination begin to flow, and questions arise naturally (Drew et al., 2008, 12). Kids wonder: What will happen if I put this here? How tall will it go? How can I keep my structure from breaking? What colors do I need to use to make green paint? In this way, constructive play serves to focus the children's minds and leads them to invent and discover new possibilities—the hallmarks of a STEM mindset.

Figure 2.8 Constructive play can happen outdoors as well.

Games with Rules

In another kind of play—games with rules—kids develop a different set of skills and strategies than in fantasy play, where children set the boundaries of play. In a game, rules are set, and in order to play the game and make the game work, you have to comply with those rules. Imagine a game of hide-and-seek where the seeker didn't cover her eyes or the hiders didn't try to find a spot where they couldn't be found. As children come to understand that they have to follow the rules or there is no game, they strengthen their self-regulation. Unlike fantasy play, where rules grow from the roles kids have taken, the rules in games usually emanate from an external source. Games with rules are often characterized by logic and order, and as children grow older they begin to develop strategy and planning in their game playing.

When playing games with rules, children also build important social skills such as cooperation and healthy competition (Elkind, 2007). They need to negotiate and work cohesively to play the game. Competition is a mighty force in human nature that playing ruled-based games can work to regulate. Understanding what it means to win and how it feels to lose is an essential part of building empathy. Games with rules can also build resilience when kids experience setbacks. Losing can be a hard thing for

Figure 2.9 Playing baseball requires knowledge of the rules.

kids (and adults). Play is the perfect venue to experience failure because children are playing with friends and not necessarily seeking approval from adults. And as we are developing a growth mindset with our students, failure can be reframed as an opportunity to learn and grow (Figure 2.9).

Rough-and-Tumble Play

Rough-and-tumble play, also known as play fighting or horseplay, is a physical form of play, which most often involves body contact between two or more children. You most commonly see this kind of play on the playground, such as children running and chasing after one another, playing tag, having sword fights, and wrestling. According to Frances Carlson, author of *Big Body Play* (2011), children most often play in these rowdy and boisterous ways with their friends, and they exhibit signs to show that they enjoy the play: "They smile and laugh, join the activity voluntarily, and readily return for more, time and time again. Their faces are free and easy, and their muscle tone is relaxed" (6). All young children and animals crave this kind of play, and it is the kind that we adults tend to get the most nervous about. We worry that kids will take it too far (which they do) or get hurt (which they do), and thus a common response is to put a stop to it. Because this type of play tends to generate a lot of controversy, yet is so crucial to the development of a healthy, happy child, it's even more important to be very clear about its benefits than with other more acceptable forms of play.

Roughhousing is necessary not only for physical development but social and cognitive development as well. According to Stuart Brown (2010), a "lack of experience with rough-and-tumble play hampers the normal give-and-take necessary for social mastery, and has been linked to poor control of violent impulses later in life" (89). For example, while studying young murderers in Texas, Brown found that one

Figure 2.10 Despite the setback of falling, the faces on these children show that they are still enjoying the play.

thing they all had in common was a lack of this sort of play when they were younger. While this example may be extreme, it shows that the skills learned in rambunctious play are essential for social-emotional well-being. When children engage in play fighting, they learn what it means to "take it too far." They learn that if they are too rough, their friends will get upset and won't want to play with them anymore. They learn how to read these subtle social cues during play and develop their skills of empathy while doing so (Figure 2.10).

They also learn the art of self-restraint. Alison has vivid memories of playing Marco Polo with her older cousin Kimmy in their grandparents' pool when she was younger. Kimmy was much faster and stronger than Alison, and when Kimmy captured Alison in the pool, she did so by dunking her underwater. This often resulted in Alison yelling and crying, Kimmy getting in trouble, and the game coming to an end. Kimmy soon learned that in order to keep the game going a little longer, she would need to play a little more gently. This kind of self-restraint, also called "self-handicapping," is represented when a more skilled and stronger playmate restrains herself so that the play can continue (Carlson, 2011).

In his book, *Free to Learn* (2013), Peter Gray says that another social-emotional benefit of rough-and-tumble play is learning how to manage one's emotions, such

Figure 2.11 Hockey can be filled with all sorts of contact, but it is also filled with opportunities to play more cooperatively with friends.

as fear and anger. He says that when children engage in this type of play, they know how to "generate the level of fear that for them creates excitement but not terror" (173). When children swing each other around wildly or push each other to the ground, they experience a physical thrill and learn that while they might feel scared in the moment, they are able to manage that feeling and overcome it. The same is true for anger. Sometimes during rough-and-tumble play, a playmate takes things too far, and someone accidentally gets hurt. The player who gets hurt might get upset but soon learns that lashing out as a response only results in a fight and an end to the play. This situation becomes an opportunity for the player to learn how to manage his emotions and communicate his feelings in a different way. For example, Alison eventually learned that it was more effective to tell Kimmy, "Don't dunk me, I don't like it," rather than cry and immediately run to tell an adult, if she wanted Kimmy to keep playing with her.

Figure 2.12 After rigorous play like this, children are ready to take on quieter tasks.

Boisterous, physical play has benefits in the classroom as well. In an article titled, "The Recess Debate," published in the *American Journal of Play* (2008), Anthony Pellegrini found that children who have breaks for recess during the school day have greater levels of attention for academic tasks. This is true for older children and adults, too; it just might look a little different. Think about the last time you did something that required a lot of focus and attention; maybe it was writing report cards or writing a paper for a graduate class. You most likely found yourself getting up every so often to get a drink of water, eat a bowl of pretzels, or switch your laundry from the washer to the dryer, all so that you could go back to concentrate on the task at hand. In much the same way, Pellegrini found that the physical play that occurs during recess helps children reenergize their nervous systems and allows their brains to concentrate more fully on cognitively demanding tasks (Figures 2.11 and 2.12).

Some Types of Play Make Us Uncomfortable

"*No guns in school!*" How often have we said those words or some variation of them as we watched a block transformed into a weapon that was aimed at other children, usually accompanied with someone yelling, "bang, bang, bang"? Teaching is a political act, and every day we bring our beliefs and values to the children we teach. Sometimes in play, we will see children acting in ways that may push against our own personal belief system.

Watching children play roughly or mimic characters in pop culture that use violence can often lead to a lament that children don't know how to play these days, but in *Play for a Change*, Stuart Lester and Wendy Russell write, "[Studies] have also shown that children have not forgotten how to play, rather that we as adults may have forgotten how to see how they are playing, or remember what it feels like" (2008, 45). It's important for adults to try to differentiate between what violent games mean to children and what they mean to adults. Children look for ways to feel powerful and strong, and play is a safe way to achieve a sense of power. From a child's point of view, violent play can be alluring. It is often the children who feel most vulnerable and powerless who use aggressive play to help them feel safe. Play is their way of sorting out complicated messages that they absorb every day. In fact, research has found that children at risk for violence show a decrease in aggressive behavior when allowed to engage in rough-and-tumble play (Figure 2.13) (Brown, 2010).

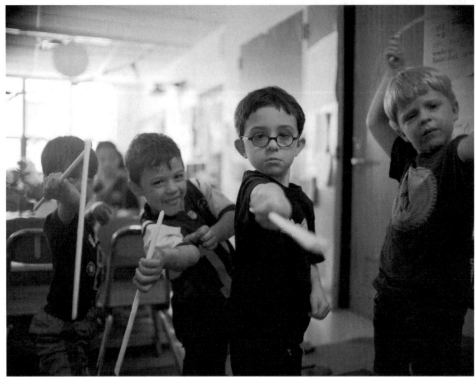

Figure 2.13 Boys playing "Power Rangers."

According to Jaye Johnson Thiel, "When we say a child 'can't play' or engage in particular narratives because those narratives aren't part of the privileged discourse, a powerful and marginalizing silence takes place in the classroom" (2014, 13). When we impose our personal, adult opinions on children's worlds created in play, we send the message that certain children do not belong because the desires and questions they bring to play are uncomfortable for adults. Yet, with or without our approval, children use play as a way to make sense of their world. Denying children a space to play in certain ways means they are left believing school is not a place for them. Consider the child whose parent may work in a bar and who wants to play "bar" in the classroom. As adults we perceive the danger of underage drinking and of the message of building and playing in a bar might send. To the child, he only knows that he wants to pretend to be like his parent, someone he idolizes and cares for, and mimic the world his family inhabits. How we respond in this situation has a lasting impact on the feelings of safety and belonging in our classroom. And, of course, we want all of our classrooms to be communities of inclusion.

It's critical for us to continually reflect on our own beliefs and values and the impact our perspective has on the children we teach. Collaborative whole-class and small-group conversations can be powerful vehicles to help children understand feelings and ideas that are confusing to them or conflict with the values of the classroom community (Figure 2.14). A conversation could start as simply as, "Let's talk about what happened today in

Figure 2.14 Risk taking on the playground.

choice time and how we feel about it." And we, as teachers, can use our experience and wisdom as powerful tools in facilitating these conversations.

Stages of Play

While children engage in many different forms of play, the type of play in each category can look different for each child, depending on his or her stage of play development. Beginning in infancy, all children progress through different stages of play. By the time they get to school, their experience level with play will dictate what stage they are in. As with all good teaching, it is helpful to have an assessment lens in mind to inform your instruction. Knowing the characteristics of each stage of play development will help you observe your students with an informed eye and move them along the developmental continuum.

One of the most iconic resources for the developmental stages of play comes from the research of Mildred Parten (1932), a sociologist from the University of Minnesota, who observed young children engaging in free play. Following her study, she categorized six stages of play, based on the children's level of interaction with one another.

Figure 2.15 This child is quite content building with Legos on his own.

- *Unoccupied Behavior*: In this most immature form of play, a child randomly observes anything that catches his interest. If nothing catches his interest, he will occupy himself by fidgeting or engaging in a repetitive behavior, such as spinning in circles or banging his hands on a table.

- *Onlooker Behavior*: The child's observations are more deliberate in nature, in that the child chooses to observe children at play. She might even approach children playing and ask them questions about their play but does not attempt to play herself.

- *Solitary Play*: As the name suggests, in solitary play a child chooses to play alone. The child might play near another group of children; however, he plays with a different toy or activity and is self-absorbed in his own play (Figure 2.15).

- *Parallel Play*: In this type of play, the child chooses to play with the same materials as another child, such as two children playing alongside one another in the block center. One child might be building a spaceship, and the other might be building a zoo. They tend not to communicate, but if they do it is to talk about what they themselves are doing (i.e., "Look at my lion!").

- *Associative Play*: In associative play children choose to play together in a group with the same materials or activity. They share materials with one another and may even decide to work on an identical project; however, there is no planning involved or organization of roles. For example, a group of children playing with blocks might decide they are going to build the Empire State Building, but each child in the group builds his or her own building.

■ *Cooperative Play:* This is considered the most mature form of play. In cooperative play, children plan how their play will go. They discuss and negotiate roles, and they role-play and dramatize scenarios. For example, a group of children might decide to build a castle in the block center. Before building they determine who is going to build the moat, who is going to build the castle, and who will work on the drawbridge. After they finish building their castle, they grab some small blocks and pretend they are knights protecting it from the enemies. In this form of play, children often need to compromise and forego their individual goals in order to sustain the play in the group activity (Figure 2.16).

In Section II of this book we offer teaching points and suggestions for how to move your children toward the more mature and cooperative forms of play. If you find you have children who are still operating in the more immature forms of play, you may need to take a step back to help move them along the continuum. Play, like all things, develops over time. Each stage offers new benefits and ways of thinking for children, and each step forward should be celebrated as growth. In all types and

Figure 2.16 These players strategize about their next step in building a gymnastics area.

stages of play, children are refining what it means to create, innovate, explore, and develop into incredible human beings.

Like a healthy diet pulls from every area of our plates, a healthy childhood pulls from all kinds of play. To develop into the fullest versions of ourselves, we need outlets for fantasy and physicality, construction and cooperation, and time to grow. Play allows children the means and the method to learn and adapt to a changing world.

3

CREATING PLAYFUL ENVIRONMENTS

*In order to act as an educator for the child, the environment
has to be flexible: it must undergo frequent modification
by the children and the teachers in order to remain
up-to-date and responsive to their needs to be protagonists
in constructing their knowledge.*

—Lella Gandini (1998),
The Italian Schools of Reggio

Louis Malaguzzi, the founder of the Reggio Emilia approach, draws a contrast between environments that speak and ones that are silent. He says that an environment that is silent doesn't really reflect the children who live and learn there, while an environment that speaks sees and reflects children's wonderings, ideas, and passions. Our environment is more than just the physical setup, though that is part of it. It is also the emotional atmosphere we generate in our classrooms and the teaching decisions we make. This chapter outlines the fundamentals of building a playful environment, from where we put our tables, to how we phrase our rules, to the way we teach our children.

If You Build It, They Will Play

How often have you set up a classroom, just so, only to find that within the first hour of the first day of school the space has been repurposed? The pillow, placed ever so delicately at a pleasing angle on the bench, is now piled with all its companions in a tower in the corner. Meanwhile, the costume jewelry from dress-up now serves as small bombs placed along the perimeter of a Lego ninja training camp. The contrast between how we, as adults, imagine how to design a space for play and learning and how children want to design a space for play and learning can be vastly different. Stuart Lester and Wendy Russell (2008) define adult-created play spaces as "places for children" as opposed to "children's places," which are spaces of children's "own making and choosing." In fact, the authors cite several studies that highlight the conflict between children's and adults' value of space, noting that adults' desire for safety, order, and visibility contrasts with children's desire for disorder, cover, loose materials, and so on. Kristi, a natural lover of order and color-coding, finds herself constantly at odds with her kindergarteners' love of stacking and piling and hoarding in no system that is clear to her. So who wins out? The answer resides in who you believe owns the space. Does the classroom belong to the teacher, or does it belong to the students?

Figure 3.1 A child makes a decoration for her classroom.

To our minds, classroom space belongs to students, but that does not mean the teacher does not have influence. How we design classrooms shows what we value, and we can design classrooms that value children's agency and right to play, while teaching into the concept of organization. We have found that considering space, materials, and routines can help adapt any classroom to one that welcomes children's needs and voices (Figure 3.1).

Space: The First Frontier

One of the few things we can control in our classrooms is the allotment of space. Though there may be some things required—for example, a rug where the whole class can gather—where each piece of furniture goes is up to us. When arranging a classroom, we suggest modifying the timeless fashion advice of Coco Chanel where she admonishes us to take one thing off before leaving the house. We advise taking one piece of furniture out before welcoming students. Less stuff will always equal a more flexible space. As all of us are former or current city teachers, we know that every square inch is precious. Here are a few things to consider when designing your classroom floor plan.

Leave Open Spaces for Children's Creations

When possible, leave open floor space where children can build and leave their structures up for multiple days (Figures 3.2). Alison's students loved to use the house they built out of cardboard boxes as a place to sit when writing or reading. What looks like unused space before school starts is actually a blank canvas for design.

In addition to sizeable plots of classroom land for big structures, explore your room for an area where works in progress can live. Creating spaces to store long-term projects sends the message that this classroom values big visions. Windowsills, countertops, and the tops of bookshelves can all house Lego spaceships, dollhouses of cardboard, and any other thing your students can dream of making (Figure 3.3).

Figure 3. 2 Open spaces allow for the building of large structures, like this first-grade rendition of a grocery store.

Figure 3.3 A windowsill is a handy repository for paintings in progress.

Like time, classroom space is precious, and teachers always wish they had more. Since your room isn't likely to magically get bigger, it helps to think critically about your furniture.

Figure 3.4 A standing table holds a Power Ranger fort in action so that children can return to it over time. Children like to sit under the table with clipboards when they need a hard space to write.

Use Furniture Flexibly

Cheryl's classroom had a hard top over the sand table that could double as a table, and Kristi's classroom had a standing table that had room for building underneath it (Figure 3.4). Rugs for whole-class meetings can double as a space for small groups to gather. Hollow blocks for building can be transformed into surfaces for writing or reading at other times at the day. Materials for play can be stored around the room so that children gather them as needed, as opposed to having a designated "blocks only" area. Using furniture flexibly, and letting go of the notion that every child needs a desk in order to learn, allows for differentiation in the environment and space for play.

Provide Different Kinds of Spaces Within the Classroom

Children like open spaces where they can move in big ways with friends and also small, cozy places to curl up and find moments of calm. The large rug meeting area can serve as a place for dance parties and epic superhero battles, but, just as important, every classroom needs a quiet, tucked-away corner. This arrangement may be as simple as putting a cushy pillow in a corner behind a bookshelf or as ornate as hanging curtains from the ceiling and partitioning off a small area with a beanbag and a lamp. What is important is finding spaces in the classroom where children can be active and loud and also quiet and calm. Though it may feel scary as teachers to have spaces in the classroom where we cannot easily see children, environmental differentiation requires us to think about the spaces we provide for children with their needs in mind.

Ask Children How They Would Like to Use the Space in the Room

Classrooms are often designed with a teacher's agenda in mind, and teachers control some spaces to ensure students have access to the things they need. However, asking children about space design invites a deeper sense of belonging to the community and opens a window into the ways children see the room. You may be bold, like second-grade teacher Christine Hertz, and leave all the furniture except the rug huddled together so that the first activity of the first day of school is a meeting to decide how to design the classroom for learning. Or you may take a more measured approach by asking children throughout the year, "What space is working for you? How else might we arrange our room to help ourselves learn?" In Alison's classroom, specific studies defined the furniture layout. Tables might be grouped to become bigger and provide more floor space for building and then break apart again as time moved on.

Extreme Makeover: Classroom Edition

Reality shows that make over people's homes often start with questions like: What do you want in a space? What do you use this room for? What do you wish you had in your home? You can do the same for yourself as you look to make over your classroom space so it invites play. Questions you may ask yourself include:

- Do I have flexible seating options (standing, sitting, laying) and the items to support that?

- Can I repurpose furniture (e.g., make tables shorter or taller, replace a regular table with a sand table with a cover) to vary the work space in the room?

- Do I have at least one largeish space where children can build and leave their buildings standing?

- Do I have at least one smallish, cozy spot for children to recenter and feel safe?

- Do I have a space in the classroom or in the hall that allows for big movement?

- Do I have materials easily available for children?

- Do I have a permanent open space to store works in progress?

- Is this environment pleasing to the eye?

Once the space has been generally established with room to move, room to build, room to save, and room to be calm and quiet, the task becomes to provision the space with materials that will inspire and ignite children's minds.

Outdoor Play Spaces

Outdoor spaces are often dictated by the presence of play structures or open spaces. Though you can't change much of the physical landscape, it is worth considering enhancing any outdoor space with options. Sandboxes and related tools for construction allow children to explore natural materials while building. Websites like Community Play Things (communityplaythings.com) and Amazon (amazon.com) sell weatherproof blocks for outdoor building (Figure 3.5). Programs like Reggio Emilia encourage using natural materials to build areas where children can make music or "cook" in a mud kitchen.

Figure 3. 5 Playing with outdoor blocks.

Figure 3. 6 A grocery basket made from pipe cleaners.

Materials: Beyond the Kitchen Set

A universal truth among small children is that they often love the box the present came in more than the present itself. A box, or a set of blocks, provides a nearly infinite amount of possibility in the imagination of a child. Just as we may love the multipurpose kitchen utensil ("A can opening–knife sharpening–lemon juicing–bottle opening–garlic grating spatula? Just what I always wanted!"), kids love open-ended materials. Play isn't made better by toys; it's made better by possibilities. In manipulating open-ended materials, like the pipe cleaners in Figure 3.6, children can solve problems and think creatively and flexibly.

In the spirit of thinking flexibly, you can use play materials as math manipulatives or materials for other parts of the day (Figures 3.7 and 3.8). They can be organized and stored in clear bins or baskets. You can decide the style of storage and the labeling of the bins without students, but inviting them into the process provides an opportunity to teach about organization and responsibility. We suggest trying to gather the following materials for your environment.

Figure 3.7 A cardboard box from a computer stands in for the real thing.

Materials for Powerful Play:

- Blocks
- Large, hollow blocks for building large structures
- Cardboard: boxes, rolls, cones, flat pieces
- Fabric for dress-up
- Paper
- Paints
- Markers, crayons, colored pencils
- Scissors
- Tape
- Staplers
- Loose parts: attractive, interesting materials
- Shells
- Rocks
- Items made of metal or wood
- Familiar objects from home/parents' workplaces

Figure 3.8 Ask parents for donations from home. You never know what you might get—like this old payphone!

Some children may need support visualizing the ways they can use such open-ended materials. Books like *Not a Box* and *Not a Stick* can spark conversations and

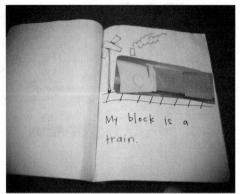

Figure 3. 9 A page from a class-made book, *Not a Block*. The text reads "My block is a train."

lead to new ways of looking at items. You may even make class books inspired by those titles to help children with inspiration (Figure 3.9).

To truly get the most out of these materials, the physical environment will bring you only so far. It is the tone of the classroom that allows children to build fearlessly, with creativity and innovation. The physical environment may be the match, but it is the emotional environment that will light the fire.

Setting the Stage for Community and Caring: Building a Play-Friendly Emotional Environment

Imagine it's September. You've just met your children, and you are certain that they will become a caring, cohesive, happy community. Of course, they're not there yet. Developing a classroom based on trust and caring is essential for play to thrive, and

Figure 3.10 A child experiments with loose parts.

it takes time. For teachers it means having a clear vision because our best teaching emanates from our deepest convictions and passions.

Think about your hopes and dreams for the children you teach. Your dreams might include independence, curiosity, and joy. Your hopes might include children who are resilient, empathetic, and able to imagine unlimited possibilities (Figure 3.10). You might dream that your children will act to fight injustice in the world. These hopes and dreams can be developed and nurtured through play. Stuart Brown says, "Play sets up the stage for cooperative socialization. It nourishes the roots of trust, empathy, caring and sharing" (Figure 3.11) (2010, 197).

According to Nell Noddings, known for her work around the ethics of caring, "Schools should become places in which teachers and students live together, talk together, reason together and take delight in each other's company" (1991, 169). When we are listening as kids engage in fantasy play, when we help them problem solve while they are attempting to build a sturdy

Figure 3.11 Sharing is an essential part of play and of communities at large.

base for their block skyscraper, when we laugh with them while they are experimenting during rough-and-tumble play, we are building a classroom community with empathy and caring as the foundation.

Create a Culture of Caring

Studies show that "if they are well fed, safe and rested, all mammals will play spontaneously" (Brown, 2010, 42). As teachers, how do we build an emotional community in our classrooms that nurtures play? And reciprocally, how do we use play to build the safe and caring community we envision? Some guiding principles that can strengthen the relationship between community and play follow:

- Get to really know each other. Play provides lots of opportunities to talk to each other about ideas, feelings, and passions and to build strong emotional bonds.

- Learn to solve conflicts by talking through them rather than tattling to the teacher. Play allows ample opportunities for this.

- Emphasize self-control and the power to positively assert oneself. Play develops self-regulation that includes the ability to make and carry out a plan, to solve a problem, to think of a good idea and act on it, to consider alternatives, and to make decisions.

- Make class meetings a forum to gather as a community to share, reflect, and problem solve. When children and teachers are able to voice opinions together, mutual respect and understanding develops.

Make Rules That Work

In *Teaching Children to Care* (2002), Ruth Charney says of rules, "The quest for rules helps us achieve our hopes. If we are going to be able to learn math, what rules do we need? If we are going to be able to make friends, what rules do we need? The rules help the good things happen." Building a classroom on a foundation of caring requires a strong infrastructure. For play to flourish, you need to establish solid structures for children based on clear expectations and rules. These rules should be in children's language, reflect their best thinking, and include common principles.

Rules Are Positive Statements

We might think back to our childhood classrooms where the rules were a litany of "don'ts." Those are the kinds of rules that are imposed by an authority and, truthfully, are often ineffective. When rules are a list of "don'ts," kids are less likely to feel free to try new things. When reactions and consequences aren't naturally related or seem arbitrary, kids can become overly fearful or just confused. So the question becomes, "How can we develop rules that require thought and participation, not merely submission?"

The purpose of rules is not to address every negative action. Rather, we want rules that are proactive and will encourage thought and discussion. In society laws and rules are necessary to ensure fairness and prevent chaos. But to live in an enlightened, productive society, just following the rules isn't enough. Along with the concept of laws and rules comes responsibility. It's our responsibility to vote, to care for those in society who are most vulnerable, to recycle. In other words, we have an obligation to act for the benefit of society at large, and we understand rules in this context.

The idea of responsibility can be imbedded in our rules. For example, we may have three positive rules in our classroom:

1. We will respect ourselves.

2. We will respect each other.

3. We will respect our classroom and the materials in our classroom.

A conversation around rules like this might include questions such as, "What does *respect* mean? What does it look like? Is it possible that roughhousing is a way to show respect to a friend in the recess yard but not in the middle of writing?" These conversations are worth having and are fundamental to creating citizens in the classroom and the world. In order to feel free to play, children need to understand the positive force of rules and to feel their ideas are respected and their desires are safe from scorn (Figure 3.12).

Rules Are Guidelines

There is a certain logic to the idea that the more specific you make a rule—"Put the blocks back on the shelf"—the more likely it is to be followed. But the logic often doesn't hold up. Even when you are very specific, kids may or may not follow a rule, depending on whether they understand the reason and purpose behind it. We believe rules are more effective when they are broad statements rather than specific ones: *We respect and take care of the materials in our classroom.* The conversations that emanate from rules like this help kids develop reasoned thinking and self-regulation and see many possibilities for positive action (instead of just one). Respecting and caring for materials means putting the blocks back on the shelf in a way that kids using them next will have easy access, but it means lots of other things too. Children will be invested in rules when they see a purpose and are part of the decision-making process.

Figure 3.12 A feeling of safety and mutual respect allows children to take risks in play and writing.

Rules Mean Specific Action

It is not enough to have a one-time discussion about the rules and then expect children to attend to them on a daily basis. Rules must become woven into the fabric of the classroom culture. We can do this by explicitly teaching them and giving positive, ongoing feedback when we notice that kids are working hard to follow them and when they need help in making better decisions. For example, a common rule during choice time is to stay in your chosen play area the whole time. A teacher might demonstrate this for the class by gathering them around her in a particular play area, such as the art center, saying, "We've been talking about how important it is to stay in one center for all of choice time, but I've been noticing that this can be hard for a lot of us to do. One way to help you stay in your center longer is to make something else when you feel you are finished." The teacher then models painting a picture and says, "I'm done. I think I'll go to blocks now. Oh wait, I can't! I need to stay in my center the whole time. OK, what else can I make?" The teacher wraps up the demonstration by reminding her students that when they feel they are done in a center, they can stop and ask themselves, "What else can I make?"

As students go off to play, the teacher moves around the room to conference with groups of them. When she notices that children are staying in their centers, she stops and names what she sees them do. For example, "Wow! I noticed that rather than finishing your block structure and trying to leave the center to go somewhere else, you decided to try to add details to make your structure even better. Do you see why it is important to stay in our centers the whole time? Look at all of this hard work you just did!" After conferring with a few more groups, the teacher gathers the class back together and tells the story of the children in the block center to highlight the strategy they used to follow the choice-time rule.

The physical and emotional environments we build help children see that they are safe and free to play. They know the classroom space is designed for their desires, and the rules and expectations insist on a culture of playful discovery.

Teaching with Independence in Mind: The Workshop Structure

Donald Graves (1985), the "father" of the writing workshop, argued that structure and predictability in the classroom are critical to the teaching of writing. He said that when children know what to expect, they are more confident and independent, and they take more initiative as learners. Most workshop teaching follows the same predictable structure, which mimics authentic real-life learning experiences. For example, if you have ever taken a cooking class, a pottery class, or a yoga class, they pretty much go the same way each time. The instructor starts out by either showing you how to do something or giving a quick talk, and then the majority of time is spent with you engaging in the action of the class, whether it is practicing your knife skills or your downward dog pose, while the instructor comes around and offers you tips. The class often closes with some sort of sharing, reflection, or celebration of the work you did. And because these workshops go the same way each time, it frees you up to concentrate on your practice, rather than worrying about what is going to happen next.

Many teachers have experienced the success of this approach in their writing workshops and have applied this method of teaching to reading, math, and other content areas. We believe that play, with its unpredictable nature, deserves to be taught in a workshop structure as well. You might be saying to yourself, "Wait . . . do I really need to teach kids how to play?" The fact is many of our students come to school with different levels and kinds of play experiences. Some students have experienced only one type of play, such as organized games and sports, and others may have spent their free time watching television or playing games on their iPad, while others engaged in endless hours of free play, building forts and castles and making mud pies. We can't assume all of our students are playing at mature levels and reaping all of the benefits that come along with that. In order to help our students learn crucial social skills and learning habits, we must give them time to play and support them in their play efforts, and a workshop structure allows us to do just that.

What Does Play Look Like in a Workshop Structure?

We believe all learning can and should feel like play. Making books in writing should have the same constructive feeling as making a block structure, and reading a book should carry the same fantastical joy as donning a superhero cape. Yet, we also think children should have time set aside purely for play, when they can pursue their own interests with the materials they choose (Figure 3.13). By attaching a workshop structure to these times, we can teach into children's play in powerful ways. Choice time and recess provide the perfect opportunities for this.

Figure 3.13 Choosing a materials center.

Choice Time Workshop

Choice time most often occurs in the classroom or in a separate room in the building dedicated to choice time, such as the Inquiry Room at PS 277 in the South Bronx where Cheryl Tyler was principal, or the upper-grade block room at PS 59 in Manhattan. During choice time children choose to play with a variety of different materials and in a variety of ways, sometimes choosing a play "theme," like "ninjas," for the duration of the day or week. A choice time *workshop* follows a similar structure to that of a reading, writing, or math workshop.

A Typical Choice Time Session*

Workshop Element	Time Frame	Description
Choosing a center or a play theme	1–2 minutes	▷ Many classrooms have a choice time board where children place their names for the day or the week. This can happen first thing in the morning or before the focus lesson.
Focus lesson	3–5 minutes	▷ Students gather in the meeting area. ▷ Teacher instructs on a strategy that supports children in play (see Section II for examples).
Planning	1–3 minutes	▷ Can be oral or written. ▷ Happens with children who chose to play in the same play area. ▷ Can happen in the meeting area before students head off to play or in the play area before they start playing. ▷ Children plan for use of materials, story lines, or characters that may be used. ▷ For more see: Porcelli and Tyler's book, *A Quick Guide to Boosting English Acquisition in Choice Time* (2008).

Workshop Element	Time Frame	Description
Work (Play) time	30–35 minutes	▷ Children are in different play areas. ▷ They stay in one area for the whole length of time. ▷ Teacher moves from group to group to talk, observe, take notes, and offer tips. ▷ If last day in center, children clean up fully; if returning to center, children neaten and organize as needed.
Share	3–5 minutes	▷ Students gather in meeting area. ▷ May teach something new, solidify previous teaching, or provide an example of something to try.

*See Appendix B for recommended time frames for choice time workshop by grade level.

Recess

Many schools have a daily recess period that comes immediately before or after lunchtime. Unless you are in a school in which teachers are required to supervise lunch and recess, many teachers are not present during this recess period and thus are not able to observe students engaging in free outdoor play. Instead, you see your students right after recess, and as their sweaty bodies pour into the classroom, so do some of their unresolved conflicts and hurt feelings. While you do the best you can to have community talks and problem-solving circles, you can't help but wonder, "What is going on out there?"

Figure 3.14 Framing questions for share sessions inspired by the book *Visible Learners* by Mara Krechevsky, Ben Mardel, Melissa Rivard, and Daniel Wilson.

Because of this, and in light of the research on the benefits of rough-and-tumble play, we recommend having an additional period of recess, so that you can observe, support, and teach into outdoor play in a more purposeful and productive way. When we have a recess period that we are able to attend, it typically goes like this.

A Typical Recess Session*

Workshop Element	Time Frame	Description
Focus lesson	3–5 minutes	▷ Students gather in the meeting area. ▷ Teacher instructs on a strategy that supports children in play (see Section II for examples).
Work (Play) time	20 minutes	▷ Children play in different outdoor play areas or with different materials. ▷ Teacher observes, offers tips, and supports play.
Share	3–5 minutes	▷ Students gather in the meeting area. ▷ Students and teacher reflect and discuss topics, such as the idea of community, empathy, and resolving disputes productively.

*See Appendix B for recommended time frames for extra recess by grade level.

Methods of Instruction Within a Workshop Structure

As with all teaching, you can choose from a variety of methods of instruction depending on your purpose. Typically we use a mix of direct instruction, inquiry, storytelling, and coaching during focus lessons, conferences, and shares in our choice-time workshops. Because each method helps children think about their play in a different way, some methods are more common to certain parts of the workshop than others.

Direct Instruction

We use direct instruction most often in our focus lessons when teaching something new to our students. The teacher names a teaching point and then demonstrates how to do it while the students watch. For example, a focus lesson on how to plan, using direct instruction as a teaching method, might sound and look like this:

> *"Today I am going to teach you how we can plan for our play together by asking each other, 'What do you want to create today?' Then we can decide which idea we will create first, or we can decide to create a mash-up by putting both of our ideas together. Watch how I do this with my partner." The teacher then uses the most common form of direct instruction, demonstration teaching, to model with a student, or perhaps another adult in the classroom, or asks two students to demonstrate while she voices over what they are doing. After the demonstration, the teacher gives the students a quick recap, naming the steps of the strategy.*

Inquiry

We typically use inquiry in our focus lessons and shares when teaching something more familiar to students. The teacher poses a question and invites students to generate the ideas and knowledge about the topic. For example, a focus lesson on how to plan, using inquiry as a teaching method, might sound like this:

> *"We have been learning a lot about ways to plan for our play. Today we are going to watch Sophie and Ben make a plan together. As we watch them let's pay close attention and think about what we notice about the way they plan and how you could use what they do in your planning today." After watching the students plan, the teacher asks the students what they notice and then records their thinking onto a chart. She then asks the students which strategies they will try in their planning today and going forward.*

Storytelling

We tend to use storytelling as a method of instruction during our teaching shares as a way to help the students relive an experience and solidify a teaching point. The teacher typically gathers students in a circle and then begins telling a story of a shared experience, one that will highlight a teaching point in some way. After the teacher begins, she invites the students to join in to continue telling the story. She encourages students to relive the moment by including details, such as dialogue and specific actions. After the storytelling experience, the teacher can either make an explicit connection to a teaching point or ask the students what they noticed or learned from the experience. For example, a teaching share on the importance of planning, using storytelling as a method, might sound like this:

"It was choice time in class 1-321. The kids in the block center decided to play 'UPS.' Lilly and Joseph grabbed some blocks and said they were going to deliver packages around the room. They started to leave the block center but then Henry and Charles said . . ." The teacher then gestures for Henry or Charles to take over. Henry steps in, *"Charles and I said, 'Hey wait, what about us?'"* Henry then called on Charles who said, *"Lilly and Joseph said that we can't all deliver packages, and Henry and I said that wasn't fair."* Joseph raised his thumb to be called on so he could continue the story. *"So then I said, 'Well, we can't really deliver without a truck!' So we all started building the truck together, and then choice time was over."*

At this point the teacher steps in and decides to make an explicit connection to the planning work the class has been doing. *"So class 1-321, did you see how Joseph and Lilly and Henry and Charles started out by making a quick plan, they said what they were going to play, but they soon realized that wasn't enough, right? They realized they needed to spend some time deciding how they were going to play 'UPS,' what they would need, and who would do which part. Without making a detailed plan their play couldn't really go anywhere because they all had different ideas about how it was going to go. So it really helps to take a few minutes at the beginning of choice time to make a detailed plan together, making sure to include not only what you are going to play but how your play will go, what you will need, and who will do which part."*

Coaching

Coaching happens most often in our conferences with students. As the name of the method implies, coaching happens from the sidelines while the play is in action (Figure 3.15). For example, if you think about a game of basketball, as the players run down the court the coach yells out short tips, such as "Guard your man!" to support the players during the game, often reminding them of things they might forget when so intensely focused on playing. The same is true when using this method during choice time. The teacher watches the children engaging in play, and when she notices they need support, she offers up some quick words of advice, and the students try it as they are playing. For example, a planning conference, using this method of coaching, might go like this:

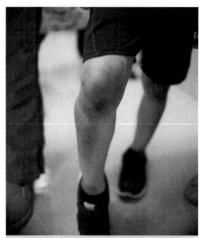

Figure 3.15 Dirty knees can mean a happy heart and a mind ready for challenge.

At the start of choice time, the teacher walks around the room and listens to the students as they plan. She stops at the dramatic play area, where the kids are talking about how they are going to play "doctor." The teacher observes and notices that Sydney, a shyer student, is passively involved in the planning. Wanting Sydney to strengthen her voice, she leans into Sydney and whispers, "Ask them, 'What do we need to make to get started?'"

Sydney turns to the others in the group and says, "What do we need to make to get started?"

Maya immediately responds, "I will need a clipboard and paper to take notes."

Sydney is quiet again so the teacher whispers to another student and says, "Ask Sydney, 'What do you need?'"

George turns to Sydney and says, "What do you need, Sydney?"

She responds, "I need a bandage and something to give a shot."

The teacher stops the group and recaps what they just did. "Did you see how you planned what you were going to do, but you also planned what you would need? Now you can spend a little time gathering and making your props and then get started on your play!"

Our environment is as much an emotional space as it is a physical one. The choices we make, from tables to rules to teaching, can have a lasting impact on the children we teach. If we truly want our classrooms to be places of joy, laughter, and vigor, where children can be children and hopes and dreams are fulfilled, then we must set the tone with our environment from the very beginning.

Play is how we become better versions of ourselves.

Section II
The Work in Play
Using Play for Social and Emotional Growth

We know play is important, critical even, and so we have shaved minutes here and there, wiggled and worked, to ensure that every single day children have opportunities to play in a multitude of ways. Your classroom is welcoming, your supplies are waiting, and you are ready to cherish play in your room. And what happens the first day? Children don't play together, or they argue. You find a box of rocks dumped on the floor, and your dreams of children building schools and stores are currently displaced by a heap of blocks in the middle of your large building area. Don't lose heart—that is how play may begin, but day after day it changes and morphs as children change and morph. We know this because we have lived it too.

There is endless learning to be done in play and chances for children to work and take action toward achieving goals. There are things to be learned about organization and valuing materials. There are things to learn about empathy and working together. There is learning to be had about resilience and optimism in life. This section will help you teach about each of those things using children's play. This section is about helping children do the work in play.

In play, we learn to care for our environment and cherish our materials.

CARING KIDS
Teaching Empathy Through Play

It is a warm spring morning in kindergarten. At drop-off, five-year-old Austin walks into the classroom, past the teacher, and straight to his friend Alena. He says, "I brought this cat for you." Alena takes one look at the picture torn from a magazine,

Figure 4. 1 This heart signals this is a community that cares about each other.

lights up, and grabs Austin for a hug. With the two words *for you,* Austin has captured the essence of empathy. He made a decision that morning to tear out an advertisement with a cat, not because he likes cats but because he knows that *Alena* does. He knows that this picture, which means little to him, will be a treasure to her, this person in his classroom whom he cares about (Figure 4.1).

Empathy is a part of every relationship and interaction and is entwined in our feelings of happiness and self-worth. Empathy is the glue that binds our world together, that allows us to look past ourselves and find others, to exist in a web struck through with threads of kindness and care. Play, in all its manifestations, is a rich and fertile ground for the development of children's social and emotional lives. This chapter will take you through reasons to linger on lessons of empathy and give you suggestions on just how to do it.

Empathy: An Exploration

The Seeds of Empathy

Empathy is our ability to feel what another person is feeling combined with an ability to take on another's perspective. Its opposite, apathy, is a lack of emotion or concern. Empathy is what helps us forge deep, meaningful relationships, and it is the reason why we care about what happens to other people (Figure 4.2). It makes us warm and connected teachers, parents, spouses, partners, and friends. All children are born with the potential to be empathic individuals, yet that ability is not always realized. Just as seeds need a certain ecosystem to grow, empathy needs certain conditions to blossom fully within us, and when nourished, it is a quality that is typically developed as we grow from infants to toddlers to young children.

The emotional aspect of empathy develops from the repeated experiences of bonding with our primary caregivers. When a baby smiles at his mother and she smiles back, a connection is formed, and he experiences feelings of love and joy. Experiencing a rich array of emotions gives us a vocabulary that we can use to read others' feelings. If you live in a world free from pain and sadness, it can be difficult to know what someone in pain is feeling. Likewise, if you have had only

Figure 4.2 Checking on a friend who has fallen demonstrates empathy.

fearful interactions, you may not know what trust feels like or what it looks like in others. Understanding an array of feelings is not enough to ensure an empathetic individual; it is only half the equation.

The other half, the perspective-taking aspect of empathy, develops from social experiences, like watching how our parents treat others, playing and fighting with our friends and siblings, and learning from our parents about recognizing right from wrong. How often have we been surprised to realize someone did not like something we liked? That failure to anticipate difference is reflective of our short-comings in perspective taking from time to time. A movie, a book, or an interaction can be different for me than it was for you. When we grasp the "you-ness," we take perspective. When a child is playing and having fun in a rough game of tag but her playmate begins to cry, that child begins to learn that how she experiences the world (I am having fun!) is different from how another might experience it (This is scary and I don't like it!). Developing both of these components—a rich emotional vocabulary and perspective taking—is essential to empathy, and depending on the circumstances, some children can develop one part of it and not the other.

If it takes two (parts) to tango, what happens when there is just one? When individuals fail to develop the dual aspects of empathy, personal, social, and societal problems can arise. Dr. Bruce Perry and Maia Szalavitz, in the book, *Born for Love: Why Empathy Is Essential—and Endangered* (2011), talk about times where the development of empathy has been disrupted or just one part has been developed. They note that autistic children often have difficulty with social relationships because they have not fully developed both aspects. While they typically can feel what others are feeling (e.g., if someone is feeling sad, they will often feel sad too), they lack perspective-taking skills (they have difficulty understanding that other people think differently than they do). For example, when Marie, an eight-year-old child on the spectrum, told Josephine that her teeth were big, Josephine became upset. Marie didn't intend to hurt Josephine's feelings, and perhaps more interestingly, she could not see why this upset Josephine, since to her it was just an observation.

Another disruption can occur when someone who has developed perspective-taking skills fails to develop the emotional aspect of empathy. When this happens, relationships suffer. These children will not experience the same feelings of joy in loving others and being loved by others. Instead, they are motivated to interact with others only if it helps them get what they want, and their perspective-taking skills make them adept at doing so. These individuals may lack moral responsibility or a social conscience and may, in the most extreme cases, develop into sociopaths (Perry and Szalaviz, 2011). In essence, the development of empathy is critical to successful social interactions and emotional well-being (Figure 4.3).

Choosing Empathy Means Choosing Play

We live in a digital world, and occasionally the tools designed to make our lives easier may have the unintended effect of interfering with the development of empathy. Cars marketed to families (minivans and SUVs) often come equipped with DVD players in the backseat. When the family takes a road trip, the children plug in and watch a movie, letting caregivers drive across country in peace. While this setup was designed to make our lives easier (and it does!!!), what is lost is the back-and-forth arguing among siblings about who is taking up too much room or who needs to roll their window down more. The resolutions of these small disputes are where empathy is forged, and when the dispute is removed, so then is the opportunity to learn and

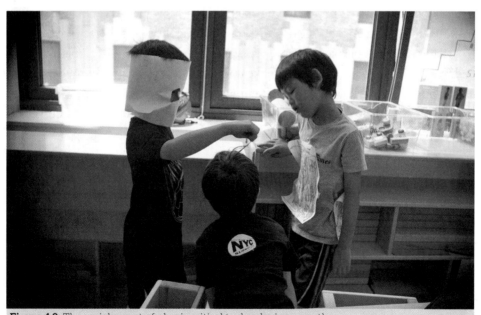

Figure 4.3 The social aspect of play is critical to developing empathy.

empathize. Using technological tools is in no way inherently evil, and when social interaction is pushed to the side occasionally, there is no long-lasting impact. Problems arise when this scenario is the *only* one children encounter, especially when the same interactions happen at school as well. Too many children come to school and encounter environments much like the backseat of this car. They are given work to do all day long that keeps them busy and quiet and away from the messy interactions that help them develop empathy. As educators we must provide opportunities for children to engage with each other and adults in a robust, social manner.

What can a teacher do? Make time for play, because play creates a space to learn how to be empathetic. In imaginative play children have a chance to practice empathy when they step into the shoes of someone else. *Undercover Boss*, a reality show on CBS, leverages the power of perspective taking. The "boss," often out of touch with her employees, goes undercover and does her employees' job for the day. After a day of cleaning out port-a-johns or flipping burgers at a fast-food restaurant, the boss realizes how hard her employees work and often rewards them by giving them raises or making their work conditions better. Role playing has the same powerful effect on children. Whether they pretend to be Superman and experience how good it feels to help others, or pretend to be Mom and see how hard it can be when their children don't clean up their messes, they are learning the skill of perspective taking.

Rough-and-tumble play is also essential for the development of empathy. When children play tag or spontaneously make up games such as "cops and robbers," they learn about boundaries, perspective taking, and give and take. As educators, it is essential that we help children develop strong hearts along with strong minds, and so we play.

Exploring Empathy in Play

Learning to be empathetic takes time, repeated experiences, and a reflective teacher to determine what might unlock a deeper sense of caring in children. Play, with its emphasis on peer interaction, is the perfect place to build empathy. These sections will serve as a tutorial of sorts, helping you think about when to focus on empathy in your classroom, what to teach to help children develop their perspective taking and enrich their vocabulary of feelings, and how to keep this work alive across the day, no matter the subject area.

We have divided this important work into two instructional areas: "Studying Faces and Bodies to Understand Emotions (My Own and Others)" and "Taking on Roles to Build Perspective Taking." These two areas are designed to address common needs in the twin aspects of empathy: understanding emotions and perspective taking.

Focus Area One: Studying Faces and Bodies to Understand Emotions (My Own and Others)

Children feel strongly. We see it in their unbounded joy at finding a small treasure and their devastating heartbreak at a friend playing with someone else. Children may experience some feelings for the first time in school. An only child may have her first pangs of jealousy. Children accustomed to success may discover frustration. Our job is not to shield children from emotions but to help them process them in healthy ways. Part of this work is helping children understand what their own emotions feel like, what they can do to manage their feelings, and how to use this knowledge to read faces and understand what others might be feeling. Building a sophisticated vocabulary of feelings is one of the primary elements in empathy.

So how do you teach children to become more empathetic? As in all teaching, the answer often resides in a close and careful study of your children. The guidelines provided in the following section are flexible and multifaceted so you can tailor them to address the particular needs of your students. We refer to them as sessions so that each individual teacher can determine the length of time needed to work on any given skill.

Possible Teaching Sessions: *Studying Faces and Bodies to Understand Emotions*

When children need	You might teach
An understanding of a range of emotions	▷ Faces and bodies tell us how other people are feeling, and we use that information to act differently. ▷ Feelings can go from big to small. ▷ Sometimes we use a word like *sad* (or *mad*) when we mean something else. Precise language helps us name and change our feelings.
Help with calming down or changing feelings from negative to positive	▷ Signs you are getting too excited: fast heart, lots of thoughts, feeling like you might explode. ▷ Strategies to calm your body: hand massage, pretzel arms, drink of water, deep breathing. ▷ You can change the message your brain is giving you: Stop and think, "What can I say to myself to change my mood?" (e.g.: It's OK, you can try again, mistakes happen, one step at a time).
An ability to "read" and react to others' faces and bodies when playing	▷ Using words to get more information: Are you OK? What do you need? How do you feel? ▷ Sort photos of faces into categories: probably OK to play, ask if OK to play, STOP!!

Lesson: What Do I Feel?

In this launching session, we ask children to act out and identify feelings in themselves and others and to pay attention to how their brains and bodies send them messages about feelings. The goal of this teaching is to help children make more empathic choices with their peers. Children often live in a world where things are absolute. If a child feels happy playing, she often assumes everyone around her is happy as well. If a child is having fun, she believes the entire group is having fun, whether or not that is the case. Teaching children to pay close attention to the faces and bodies of their peers helps them understand that their own experience may not be the experience of the group. In addition, many children need practice attaching a feeling to a particular face or action. When children are able to identify a feeling in themselves, they are more capable of seeing and naming that feeling in others and acting in empathetic ways. After Kristi had the experience of being a lost tourist in Europe, she began offering help to any person hunched over a New York City map because she knew what it felt like to be a stranger in a strange land.

Materials:

- Chart paper with the categories: face, body, brain, "I need . . ." (see Figure 4.4 for one version)
- Close-up photos of children's faces showing a range of feelings: happy, sad, angry (Figures 4.5–4.9)
- Photos of children's bodies posing to show a range of feelings: happy, sad, angry (Figure 4.10)

Procedure (8–10 minutes):

1. Gather the class, and introduce the concept: "We have feelings that make our bodies and faces look and feel certain ways. When we know how we feel, it helps us to be in control."

2. Show one photo of a face, and ask children, "What feeling could this show? Why do you think that?"

Figure 4.4 A co-created "How Do You Feel?" chart with drawings instead of pictures.

Figure 4.5 A chart that shows a range of feelings.

Figure 4.6 A chart that names feelings similar to sad.

Figure 4.7 An "I feel—I need" chart designed by teacher Kathryn Cazes.

Figure 4.8 A hallway space is dedicated to body breaks for calming and recentering.

Figure 4.9 This personalized chart, made by teacher Kathryn Cazes, offers strategies for changing your mood.

Figure 4.10 A chart to check, "Is someone OK to play?"

3. Attach the photo to the chart and annotate.

4. Have the children try to replicate the feeling in their own face and name times when they have felt that way. Repeat with the other face and body photos.

5. Once the face and body photos have been annotated (quickly), ask for thoughts on what your brain might say to you when you feel that way. Record responses on the chart.

6. Link to play by asking children to pause and do a body and brain check when they go off to play. Children do not see their own faces, so their best sense of feelings may come from those two sources of information.

End of Play Share Possibilities:

- Underscore the causal relationship of action and feeling by asking children to try out this sentence with an example from their play: "I felt _____ when _____ happened."

- Ask children to share a moment when they realized how they were feeling and how they knew.

- Role-play other feelings not yet on the chart.

Our hope is that this quick outline of a lesson will help you begin to visualize how this instruction might unfold in your classroom. We know actual examples are important, too, so the following "Peek Inside the Classroom" is the first of several sections you'll find throughout the book that show you actual teaching scenes from classrooms dedicated to play. In each example, we pause to notice and name the important moves each teacher is making to help you think about the scene with more intention.

Peek Inside the Classroom

Direct Instruction:
Reacting to Faces: Asking, "Are You OK? What Do You Need?"

For this lesson, Yvonne has gathered her class in a circle on the rug. The children have chosen their centers already and have a plan for what they will play. However, today's lesson will be focused on what happens once the play starts. Yesterday, Yvonne noticed that some kids were becoming the "boss" of a play situation by assigning the others roles. Cullen, Arjun, and Jadon loved playing "Transformers." Arjun had clearly taken on the role of "boss" over the past several days and was clear about who would play the good Transformers and who would play the bad Transformers. Cullen joined in the game but seemed sad, and his usual spirited engagement was missing. Yvonne had talked a bit to Cullen and found out that he hated being the bad guy, yet Arjun kept assigning him that role. It turns out Arjun could tell that Cullen was mad, but he felt there was a greater need for the "bad guys" in the center.

Before the lesson begins, Yvonne chooses two students, Avery and Jenny, to role-play in front of the class. Yvonne preps them for the lesson by saying to them, "You are going to pretend you are playing in blocks together and things don't go so well. Pretend to do the things I say."

Notice How…

* The teaching point came from some trouble that had arisen during choice time. Observing students closely during choice time and free play helps us determine meaningful and timely teaching points and learn about our students' strengths and needs in less-structured settings.
* Students chose their centers prior to the lesson so they can focus on the lesson and make a smooth transition when it is done.

Yvonne begins the lesson: "Friends, we have been working on watching friends' faces when we play to see if they are OK to play. Remember, we know our friends are OK to play when they are smiling or laughing or have a calm face."

Yvonne gestures to the feelings chart. "Yesterday I noticed that some friends had faces that looked sad or mad, but nothing happened to help those friends change their feelings! When we have empathy, we don't just let our friends feel bad, we take action! One thing we can do is ask our friends, 'Are you OK? What do you need?' and then we can find out what we can do to make it better. Let's watch this in action with Avery and Jenny."

Yvonne drops a few blocks on the rug and invites Avery and Jenny to the center of the circle to "pretend like they are playing." Avery and Jenny begin to build, and then suddenly Avery grabs a block out of Jenny's hand, and Jenny scrunches up her face.

The class begins to giggle, and Yvonne steps in to voice-over what is happening. "Jenny's face looks different now. Instead of smiling she started to frown and scrunch up her forehead. Avery knows friends look at other friends' faces for clues about how they are feeling. So right now Avery is thinking, "I think Jenny feels . . ."

The class jumps in and names the feeling: "MAD!!" In response Jenny clenches her fists, further committing to her role.

Yvonne stops everyone, "Let's push pause on this movie. Avery could keep building, but that would not show empathy toward Jenny. Jenny should check in with her friend and ask, 'Are you OK? What do you need?' Let's try that. I am going to hit play. Avery, ask Jenny."

Avery checks in and finds out that Jenny is, in fact, mad that she took her blocks, but Jenny is unsure what she needs.

Yvonne stops one more time to ask, "What action could Avery take now? Turn and tell your neighbor." Yvonne names out options she hears from the class—give the block back, find another block, ask if she can use it—and says, "Avery can ask which of those things Jenny would like. Try it, Avery!" Avery offers a menu of choices to Jenny, who chooses to let her borrow the block.

Notice How...

* Role play was used to teach, allowing the rest of the students to have a bird's-eye view of a common scenario.
* The observations were directed by the teacher's voice-over.
* Reflection was built in through the opportunities to turn and talk.

Yvonne hits pause on Jenny and Avery one more time. "Friends, when we see faces that look like they may not be having fun in our choice time center, we check in and ask: 'Are you OK? What do you need?' And if we need to take a different action to help our friend, we can!"

Over the next few days, the first graders practiced this as Yvonne snapped photos of "checking in and making changes" to talk about in the share.

Notice How...

* Photographs document students' progress with the skill, making the chart more meaningful and user-friendly for students.

Reflection and Next Steps:

Yvonne is carefully taking notes during choice time to get a sense of how first graders are handling this skill of stopping their own play to check on a friend. As she watches she notices children toss out the word "sorry" like a magic spell to fix things and decides she needs to spend some time with her class thinking about diverse ways of handling and resolving problems.

Focus Area Two: Taking on Roles to Build Perspective Taking

Though understanding feelings is an essential part of empathy, it is only half the equation. Empathy also requires stepping into another's life fully. It can be easy to assume that another person has the same inclinations and reactions we have, but rarely, if ever, does that bear out. In teaching children to take on roles, we teach them to stretch outside of themselves, sample the world from another's point of view, and see how it might be different (Figure 4.11). When a role play is over, our experience as that person still remains, widening our understanding of the world.

We believe that the more support we give children to fully embrace a role as another person, the more deeply they experience the feelings that lead to empathy. To that end, the following sessions teach children how to step into another's life as fully as possible. Though most of this instruction takes place in the realm of children's fantasy play, it lays an essential foundation for perspective taking in everyday life.

Figure 4.11 A little bit of paper and this kindergartener is now a knight.

Possible Teaching Sessions: *Taking on Roles to Build Perspective Taking*

When children need	You might teach
Support talking like other characters in order to better understand their perspective	▷ Common language of certain roles: family members, friends, waiters, cashiers, doctors. ▷ Observing closely by watching videos, taking trips, and reading books to take on the language and catchphrases of characters [Figure 4.12].  **Figure 4.12** A chart capturing the ways different characters may use language.
Help transforming their appearance to better understand another's perspective	▷ Different ways to manipulate art materials [Figure 4.13]. ▷ Studying photos bit by bit to get small details on costumes.  **Figure 4.13** Blocks stand in for a skateboard in this simple transformation.

continues

continued

When children need	You might teach
Help transforming their actions to better understand another's perspective	▷ Storytelling with fairy tales and fables and asking, "Why did the character do that?" ▷ Name that character! Teacher gives a role to a child, and the child silently acts it out until someone guesses who he is. ▷ Acting activities: walk like a rock star, sit like a queen, imitating characters in books children love (Figure 4.14).

Figure 4.14 Pictures illustrate the ways actions help transform a character.

When children need	You might teach
Using perspective taking to better understand others	▷ Reflection questions: What do I know now? How does this make me see the world differently? How might I act differently now?

Lesson: Transform Yourself! Who Will I Be? How Will I Look?

In the words of mothers everywhere, "Dress for the job you want, not the job you have," meaning, if you have an aspiration, it helps to have a costume to help you visualize reaching it. This attempt to no longer be you but to live for a few moments as someone else is trying out perspective taking. This skill is what enables adults to say, "Ah, I can see it from your point of view."

Children have always loved to wear costumes because it gives them another identity. This session sets up children to think about the clothing and tools they will need to play a role, and the share at the end brings this play into the real world. Costumes and tools are important for young thinkers to make a transition into acting differently; the concrete act of wearing another's clothes can help very young children make more abstract empathetic insights. Balancing a waiter's tray illustrates that the job is more complicated than it may first appear. Dressing up like Mom or a big brother or sister will help kids begin to understand the feelings of their parents and siblings. Just as new workout clothes may help you see yourself as more of an athlete, making and using costumes and tools help children see themselves as someone else for a little while, and then they use that knowledge to interact differently with the world. Children are literally walking in another person's physical and mental shoes.

Materials:

- Open-ended materials: fabric, cardboard, paper, and so on
- Pictures of people/characters in popular play themes: Teenage Mutant Ninja Turtles, storeowners, police, family members, friends.

Procedure (8–10 minutes):

1. Gather students together and introduce the concept: "When we play, we often pretend to be other people, acting and talking how they would talk. One thing we can do to feel even more like the person is to dress like them by making clothes and tools that make us look and feel like them."

2. Spread the art materials and fabric so children can see them. Ask, "How could we use these materials to become _____?"

3. Have children turn and talk to strategize how they might transform themselves using the open-ended materials.

4. Share out ideas: The fabric could become clothes that moms/teachers/friends wear; the flattened cardboard box could be a waiter's tray—or a changing table for a baby!

5. Link to play saying, "Today, think about how to use the materials in the classroom to help you really *feel* like the person you are pretending to be."

Possible Ending Shares:

Empathy flourishes when we communicate authentically on an emotional level. By sharing feelings, opinions, and ideas we are able to relate to and understand each other. Encourage kids to:

- Reflect: How did you feel wearing different clothes and using specific tools? Was it different from just being yourself?

- Reflect: Did becoming another person help you understand that person's feelings? How?

- Develop further: How could we change our voices and the words we say to become another person?

- Transfer our learning to our reading and writing: How does this help us understand the characters in the books we are reading and the stories we are writing?

Is It Done? Are We Empathic Yet?

Developing empathy, like nearly everything in life, is a recursive process. At various times children (and adults, too!) are ready to process and understand the world slightly differently. Teaching into empathy is never done. Rather, it is something you and your children revisit as they grow and change throughout the year, year after year, as it becomes an intrinsic part of the classroom community. However, there will be times when you are more "on" the topic as a class, and times when you are "off" it, much like how a theme in music rises and retreats across a song or soundtrack. These sessions can be shortened at one point in the year and revisited at length later or vice versa. Your children may show you a need to veer in a different direction, and if that is the case, we urge you to follow them there. Even when play moves to a different focus, the echoes of the empathy work children have done will linger in other curriculum areas.

Let's Act and Make a Difference!

It is not enough to be compassionate, we must act.

—The Dalai Lama

Nel Noddings (2013), an educator whose career has focused on ethics and moral education, describes two types of caring. Natural caring is person to person, beginning with parent to child. Ethical caring is for ideas, knowledge, and social causes; living life with a purpose. As we teach children to be empathetic, we also want them to understand the importance of acting on their beliefs and becoming involved in social activism. Activism is a powerful tool for learning because it helps kids to engage with and apply what they've learned about empathy through play while developing a deeper sense of fairness and social justice.

For example, after a particularly contentious recess with their second-grade classmates in the South Bronx, Jasmine and Nelly went to their teacher, Joe Weaver, for help. Joe listened as the girls brought up the issues that happened on the playground: kids not listening to one another's requests to stop, kids being left out of games, and arguments erupting over who was really best friends. Faced with this litany of issues, Joe saw the girls were genuinely upset over how their community was interacting, and he decided to teach how empathy leads to action. Joe sat the class down for a conversation and said, "When you are a person with empathy, you can see things that don't feel right or fair. It is up to us, the community, to come up with an action that can start to fix that. What can we do to make a powerful change at recess?"

Teaching children that change occurs because of a series of intentional actions is the basis of creating socially conscious individuals. Rather than solving the problem for the class, Joe's trust that the community can work together to create change communicates a much bigger and more critical issue: "You have the power to make a difference." The roots of social action begin first as fighting for justice in the classroom community. Joe facilitated the conversation, always harkening back to the idea that things were not fair, and the action would have to make things more fair for everyone in the community. Eventually the classroom decided to create a Caring Committee that would keep an eye out for problems at recess and other times during the day and seek to intervene. They set up guidelines for themselves and for future members:

- If new kids join the class (which often happened because of the temporary housing shelter), they would be their special friends at lunch, recess, or whenever they were needed.
- If visitors joined the class, they would make a plan to make them feel welcome.

continues

continued

- If someone was feeling sad or had hurt feelings, they would take special care of that person, try to find out why, and act to do something about the problem.
- As members of the committee, they would work especially hard on always being inclusive and caring.

The Caring Committee sowed the seeds for social activism for the second graders of class 2-203 as they learned to transform their empathy and compassion into social action.

Teacher Takeaway: When problems arise around issues of empathy (or lack thereof), resist the urge to solve them. Instead, facilitate a community conversation that puts the power of action in the hands of the children.

Curriculum Connections: Empathy

Though we may start to work on empathy during choice time because of the rich social and emotional opportunities inherent in play, empathy has its tentacles in all aspects of the school day. Capitalizing on the foundation you have built in play will make these transitions to academics powerful and rich and more meaningful to children.

Reading

The skills of inference and interpretation have quite a bit to do with a reader's own emotional vocabulary and personal experience. The more rich a child's emotional experience, the more depth he can bring to a text. The lessons of studying a person in real time to see how they are feeling translate beautifully to character studies and discerning the nuances of character development. "How do I feel?" easily becomes "How does my character feel?" The close study of bodies and faces in choice time will become children's source of evidence in texts. Role-playing during choice time helps children more easily understand point of view in text and the very tricky idea that narrative is not objective truth: It is one character's interpretation of the events.

Writing

In writing, teachers often struggle to help children become more elaborate writers and move from summary to storytelling. Choice time work on empathy creates a rich tapestry of understanding around how people act when they feel certain ways or take on certain roles. Referring back to the feelings chart created in choice time can help children move into showing (and not telling) how a character feels, as well as being more precise in vocabulary. Role-playing in choice time can support dialogue and story development in both true and imaginative stories. In fact, choice time itself is a story-generating machine. Children who say they have no ideas have a score of possibilities when they engage in powerful fantasy play (Figure 4.15).

Figure 4.15 Making character puppets supports writing realistic fiction.

Social Studies

The beauty of social studies is that it provides a steady stream of opportunities to widen children's understandings of the world. For example, on a class trip to a local store during a study of community, children can study the real-world roles of workers. Back at choice time, a teacher can use notes, photographs, and even videos from the trip to help children better take on a role and replicate what they have observed. The learning that happens when children bring the world back to their play is reciprocal in nature. In role-playing a community worker's job, for example, a child will better understand the social studies content and develop more questions and wonderings.

As Dr. Bruce Perry and Maia Szalavitz say, "If we don't practice empathy, we can't become more empathetic. If we don't interact with people, we can't improve our connections with them" (2010, 289). We cannot underscore how important it is to create space in our curriculum to help children develop this crucial life skill. When we invest time into teaching into empathy, we not only build a more caring classroom community, we help our students develop into compassionate human beings. Play is at the heart of all of this.

5

PLAYING TOGETHER

Teaching Kids to Collaborate and Negotiate

Alone we can do so little; together we can do so much.
—HELEN KELLER

It is entirely possible to be with people, and yet never really *be* with them. Think of coworkers sitting back-to-back in a silent cubicle, children playing side-by-side in the block center without a word among them, and learners struggling with a math problem within the confines of their own desks. Physical closeness and casual conversations are not the same as collaboration. We sometimes think of ourselves as closed-circuit beings, wholly self-sufficient on our own, when really we are more akin to the atoms inside of everything: better when interconnected. Through connection and collaboration we can create something bigger and greater and more important than what we could ever create alone.

Yet, few things are as challenging for people as collaboration and negotiation, which require a subsuming of the "I" to build something as a "we." They require empathy and negotiation, active listening and mutual respect, and a shared and meaningful goal. Continued collaboration requires the motivation of a payoff for each participant that is greater than what could be achieved alone, and play can be fertile ground for successful collaborative outcomes (Figure 5.1).

Figure 5.1 Collaboration is essential for cleaning up when the work has been epic.

Through working together and negotiation, children can build taller block structures, play more intricate games, plan and create new scenarios, and build a skill set essential for a successful and fulfilled life.

Collaboration: An Exploration

According to the Common Core State Standards, in order for students to demonstrate college and career readiness, they must be able to work and communicate with other people in an effective way (NGA & CCSSO, 2010). While twentieth-century jobs valued competitiveness and top-down organizational structures (think of the movie *Wall Street* and other characterizations of success in the '80s), today there is a shift toward collaboration, relationships, and shared purpose. If everyone is not pulling on the same end of the rope, quality and productivity suffer.

This is true for businesses, such as Apple and Citibank, as well as for doctors, lawyers, and teachers. In a research study conducted in 2011, University of Pittsburgh professor Carrie R. Leana found that collaboration with colleagues around student instruction is not only an essential part of every teacher's job but something that results in rising student achievement. Successful schools often arrange prep schedules so that teachers can have common periods to work and plan together each week. As teachers, we value working together because we know our most productive thinking happens when we can bounce ideas off one another, offer various experiences and perspectives, and lend our colleagues a critical eye.

Collaboration enhances student learning as well. If you walk into many classrooms today, you will not see desks in rows but rather tables with four to six students working together, solving problems, negotiating conflicts, and learning from each other. A culture of collaboration has become an essential component of a successful school much as it has become a requirement in the twenty-first-century workplace. But what exactly is collaboration? It is more than just cooperation—the "sure, we can do it that way" approach. It is about something bigger—the "and what if we tried this way instead?" approach. Collaboration is an action, a way of approaching others with the attitude that thinking together will always yield more results than thinking alone.

Play Means Learning to Collaborate

In order to collaborate with others effectively, a person needs to have developed what Howard Gardner calls "interpersonal intelligence." Howard Gardner, who developed the theory of multiple intelligences (1993), and his colleague Thomas Hatch (1990) define interpersonal intelligence as the ability to organize groups of people around a common goal, prevent or resolve conflicts, negotiate solutions, and make personal connections with others by recognizing and responding to others' feelings (empathy) (Figure 5.2). In other words, individuals with interpersonal intelligence are the Ferris Buellers of the world—the kinds of people we like to be around. They are often successful leaders in their chosen careers and lead rich personal lives with meaningful relationships.

While some people seem to naturally excel in this area and are socially savvy from a very young age, interpersonal/social skills are not a fixed set of traits. They are skills that, when tended to, can be developed and strengthened over time. In his book, *Free to Learn*, Peter Gray (2013) explains that the best place to teach children social skills is through play. "Play is nature's way of teaching children how to solve their own problems, control their impulses, modulate their emotions, see from others' perspectives, negotiate differences, and get along with others as equals. There is no substitute for play as a means of learning these skills" (175). Gray argues that this rings true for self-chosen and self-directed free play but not for sports and activities organized by adults. For example, consider a game of tag that children spontaneously decide to play during recess. The children decide who is going to be "it" first, they determine who the characters in the game will be (will they be cops and robbers today, or will they be good ninjas and bad ninjas?), and they let each other know when the play is getting too rough. When children engage in self-initiated, collaborative play with others, they determine the rules and make the necessary compromises to keep everyone happy and playing.

Figure 5.2 A difference in opinion about how to build this structure gives rise to negotiation and compromise.

Sports and adult-organized activities do not allow children the same opportunities to develop these skills because the rules are already created, an adult handles the conflicts, and the roles are assigned. There is nothing wrong with these activities, of course. It's just that they are not a replacement for free play. Children need a balance of both kinds of recreation so they have opportunities to develop these crucial lifelong interpersonal skills.

Collaboration Means Learning to Self-Regulate

In addition to interpersonal skills, collaborative play has many other benefits. When children engage in collaborative play (as opposed to nonsocial types of play, such as parallel play), they balance their needs with their playmates'. For example, a child might want to build the *Millennium Falcon* with his friends, but his friends have already decided they are going to build a police station. Most likely, the child will need to suppress his desire to play Star Wars so he can play with his friends. Or alternatively, his friends might decide that the *Millennium Falcon* can be housed at the police station so they can all play together (Figure 5.3). Either way, the children are learning the art of self-restraint in order to sustain their play. This kind of

Figure 5.3 These friends decided to add a seat to the motorcycle so they could both ride.

self-regulation is a necessary life-skill in order to control our emotions and have willpower. Self-regulation helps us say no to eating yet another Girl Scout cookie or walk away rather than saying something hurtful when we feel upset. Children often learn self-restraint for the first time when they engage in collaborative play.

Collaboration Means Learning to Communicate

Language learning is also enhanced when children engage in collaborative play. As children take on different roles, make up different rules, and negotiate with their peers, they try on different language structures (Weisberg, Zosh, Hirsh-Pasek, Golinkoff, 2013). For example, when a child tries to convince her friends to let her be the doctor, she practices the language of persuasion. While she pretends to be the doctor, she draws upon her experiences from the doctor's office and reaches for the language needed to carry out the role—"Let me take your temperature." Immersed in the sounds of social language, English language learners benefit tremendously from collaborative play. "As children build, act and draw, they are also talking about what they are doing; the hands-on work provides them with a context for all their spoken language" (Porcelli and Tyler, 2008, 17).

In order for children to learn the skills of collaboration and thus reap the benefits of it, we must provide space and time for them to do so. The next section outlines ways we can use all types of play to develop these skills.

Exploring Collaboration and Negotiation in Play

The social nature of play is a natural catalyst for collaboration and negotiation. Though children should spend some time on their own, pursuing personal interests, there are also times when playing together is richer and more joyful. A child's world of superheroes increases in dimension when there is a teammate to battle with, just as playing "restaurant" becomes more engaging when you have customers to serve. As in previous chapters, these sections serve as a tutorial of sorts, helping you think about when to focus on collaboration and negotiation in your classroom, what to teach to help children develop their collaborative skills, and how to keep this work alive across the day, no matter the subject area.

All classrooms, Pre-K–3, should consider collaboration and negotiation a primary goal of play sessions. Depending on the children and grade you teach, however, your expectations and the timing of your teaching will differ. For the most inexperienced children, simply sharing items may be the first goal, but as children gain comfort and familiarity with problem solving and the benefits of playing together, your lessons will reflect that sophistication. We have found negotiation and collaboration to come up naturally in free and fantasy play and more systematically when the idea of planning for play is introduced and expanded.

Focus Area: Playing Together Means Working and Thinking Together

Within the first five minutes of the first day of school, you will have a sense of what your students know about working together. From figuring out where to sit on the rug to negotiating the lunchroom, whenever children have choices to make, you will see their burgeoning sense of collaboration and negotiation. Inevitably these two concepts will come up before children make it to recess on the first day, so you are certain to have general classroom routines to support them as they problem solve. Yet, in play, the stakes are often raised for children. Negotiations with another child are heightened when the payoff is who gets to play Robin and who gets to play Batman. The following teaching sessions (see Figures 5.4–5.9) provide explicit ways to encourage effective collaboration and negotiation but also call on a whole host of other skills: resilience, flexibility, communication, and, of course, empathy. Much of this work will happen during the planning stage of each play session but also as need arises within play.

Possible Teaching Sessions: *Playing Together Means Working and Thinking Together*

When children need	You might teach
Basic problem solving	▷ Problems come in different sizes and need different solutions.
	▷ Using "I" messages.
	▷ Using a problem-solving chart or a classroom "peacekeeper."
	▷ Simple ways to solve disputes: rock, paper, scissors; eenie, meenie, miney, moe; flip a coin (or a counter).
More sophisticated conversational skills (listening, clarifying, disagreeing politely)	▷ Rules of active listening (eyes on speaker, head nodding, restating).
	▷ Questions to get more information: Can you say that again? Did you mean _____?
	▷ Sentence frames to agree/disagree/add on.
Help collaborating within a center	▷ Making a to-do list for the jobs in a center.
	▷ Looking at books for story ideas and negotiating roles from the book.
	▷ Varied planning sheets to problem solve ideas and roles before the play starts.

Figure 5.4 One example of a problem solving chart inspired by The Autism Project of Illinois.

Figure 5.5 An "I" message chart made by teacher Katie Lee.

Figure 5.6 Classrooms can build expectations for conversations.

Figure 5.7 Sentence frames can support whole-class conversations.

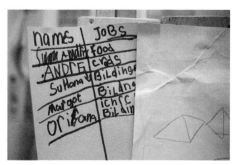

Figure 5.8 A student designed to-do list for a center.

Figure 5.9 A sample choice time planning sheet from first grade

Lesson: Planning for Roles and Jobs Within a Play Session

In this session, we ask children to plan ahead who will do what job or play which role as an exercise in collaboration and negotiation. It may be helpful to pull from a personal or class experience ("My sister always got to be the manager of the store, and I never did!") to underscore the need for loose planning ahead of time. Depending on your students, this session could be done orally or with a quick jot. The real work of collaboration and negotiation comes from working out the disagreements that might arise and problem solving solutions so that everyone gets what they want eventually. Teaching simple, quick, and effective ways to solve disputes will come in handy all day long.

Materials:

- planning sheets (see Figure 5.10)
- sticky notes
- pens

Procedure: (8–10 minutes)

1. Gather the class so children are sitting with the classmates they will play with in their chosen centers. Introduce the concept with an explanation. "Sometimes when we play, people want to have the same jobs or the same roles, or there are not enough jobs and roles for everyone. Planning ahead can help us tackle these problems before we start!"

2. Show role/job-planning sheets, and explain how they are used. "On each sticky note, write a role, and make a sticky note for all the roles you'll need. On the planning sheet, write the names of all the people you are playing with, and then decide who will have each role."

3. Have children start working on the rug. Keep eyes peeled for when there are not enough jobs or if children want the same job. If you see an issue, stop and ask students, "How can we solve this and still be fair?"

4. If you don't see any issues with the negotiation of roles, stop the class and ask, "What could we do if more than one person wants the same job?"

5. For either question, record possible solutions on chart paper, possibly calling it "Have a Problem to Solve?" and offer a few possibilities that are not named: play rock, paper, scissors; switch roles each day; make two of one role or job; look at a book to find more roles or jobs for the center.

Figure 5. 10 The Ninjago center sorts out who will get to be Kai.

6. Link to play by saying, "You can change your roles at any time by just moving around the sticky notes. If your team runs into trouble while playing, look back to your planning sheet, and talk it out using some of the solutions we came up with."

End-of-Share Play Possibilities:

- Ask children to set up a planning sheet for the next day based on who played today.

- Add to the "Have a Problem to Solve?" chart started in the focus lesson.

- Ask, "When are other times during the day when you might need to plan ahead with friends?"

It can sometimes be challenging to picture moving from the page into practice, so to that end, once again let's peek inside a kindergarten classroom working on collaboration and negotiation during play sessions.

Peek Inside the Classroom

Coaching: Negotiating Roles in a Play Theme

It was March in Kristi's kindergarten class, and the children had progressed from signing up for an area of the classroom to play in, such as blocks or dramatic play, to proposing various play themes, such as playing "restaurant" or "beauty salon." After teaching a planning lesson about roles, Kristi's students scurried off the carpet to their various play theme groups around the room. Children had proposed these centers and voted on the ones they would play in this week. Checking in quickly, Kristi saw the "Chuck E. Cheese" group had a good plan for who was going to do what, and now they were using cardboard boxes to build another ride. The "Birthday Party" group had already decided who was going to be which person at the party and were in the middle of making a plan for what was going to happen.

"Maybe we should go to Chuck E. Cheese!" someone exclaimed.

Kristi moved over to the Ninjago group and noticed that Oliver had his head down on the planning sheet, while the other two boys in the group, Eric and Marco, were busily talking about their Ninjago plans, seemingly unaware that Oliver was upset.

Notice How . . .

* Check-ins are quick at each center.
* Check-ins help you gather information about how students handle conflicts and offer many opportunities for coaching.

Kristi sat down at the table and asked, "Hey, Ninjago Team, can I see your plan and see who you are all becoming?"

Oliver, with a sad face quietly said to Kristi, "I don't want to be Morro."

Kristi responded loud enough so the other group members could hear, "Sounds like you need to tell that to the people in your center. Be brave—tell them what you are thinking." Eric and Marco stopped what they were doing and turned around to face Oliver and Kristi.

Oliver pleaded, "I don't want to be Morro. I want to be somebody else."

Kristi leaned over to Eric and Marco and whispered, "Ask Oliver, 'Who do you want to be?'"

Eric asked Oliver, "Who do you want to be?"

Oliver repeated, "I don't want to be Morro." Kristi looked to Eric and Marco and gestured with her arms, as if to say, "What should we do now?"

Eric and Marco took the bait and began offering ideas to Oliver. "You could be Zane." Eric said.

Marco added, "Or you could be Sensei Wu!"

Oliver, still looking defeated said, "I don't want to."

Marco, trying to make Oliver feel better, offered, "Sensei Wu is the strongest!" While the boys offered ideas, Kristi jotted down some notes for herself in her conference binder.

Oliver looked to the boys and got up the courage to say what he had wanted to tell them all along: "I want to be a Power Ranger Ninjago."

Marco and Eric looked at each other and then said to Oliver, "There is no Power Ranger Ninjago."

Oliver, looking sad again, said, "But I want to."

Notice How . . .

* Students are prompted to take on the language and actions of problem solving (rather than the teacher doing it), giving them confidence to do so in the future.
* The teacher's voice is not the most dominant—like a baker checking rising dough, stepping in only when needed and letting nature take the lead.
* The teacher jots notes during a conference to capture observations, to help find patterns and guide teaching.

Kristi stepped in to give the boys another strategy for problem solving. "People don't always have to stick to the rules of exactly how it is in a book when you play. If you decide as a team that it could be cool to have a new kind of Ninjago, a Power Ranger Ninjago, you could do that. So Oliver, you could try asking, 'Hey, could we try having a Power Ranger Ninjago?'" Oliver looked to the boys, waiting for them to answer. Kristi, wanting Oliver to solve the problem himself, whispered to him, "So try asking, 'Can I be a Power Ranger Ninjago?'"

Oliver turned to the boys and said, "Can I be a Power Ranger Ninjago?"

The boys shrugged their shoulders and replied, "Yeah, OK." Oliver smiled and looked relieved.

As she stood, Kristi said, "Did you see that? Your friends listened to you when you asked. Sometimes all you need to do is ask, and your friends will know what you need. And remember, as a group you can make up your own rules for how you want your play to go and what the different roles can be, just like you just did by making a new kind of Ninjago character. That is one of the cool things about play—we get to invent things." The boys excitedly made a plan for what was going to happen in their Ninjago play that day and then got started.

Notice How . . .

* The teacher called attention to the positive consequences of the child's actions (your friends listened to you).
* The big idea was stated in a clear, concise way, and the strategy was generalized so students can remember it and apply it to different situations in the future.

Letting Children Lead—The Roots of Social Action

I am only one, but still I am one. I cannot do everything, but still I can do something. And because I cannot do everything, I will not refuse the something that I can do.

—Helen Keller

Sometimes collaboration and negotiation are challenging, not because of what is said but because of what is unsaid. Helping children identify who is being excluded and finding ways to include everyone is an essential aspect of building a collaborative community.

Lauren and Justin teach a second-grade inclusion class, meaning 40 percent of the class has disabilities. One of their main goals for the year was for their children to understand that the foundation of collaboration, negotiation, and empathy was about living inclusive lives. Their exploration into critical literacy began as a result of careful listening and conferring during choice time when a group of children decided that their play theme would be "school," a popular and often-played topic.

The group collaborated, made a plan, and decided that Samuel would be the teacher that day. Samuel selected the class's favorite picture book, *Everyone Can Learn to Ride a Bicycle* by Chris Rascha, to read as a read-aloud to the rest of the group. Lauren and Justin had introduced the book to the class to open the conversation that as learners, persistence and determination can help you achieve big goals. Samuel read the book and then asked his students to form a circle for the "book conversation," mimicking what they had been doing for months in their own classroom.

Maritza started with a thought she had had for a while, saying, "I don't think this book is true." After receiving a few puzzled looks, she continued, "Well, look, it says, 'First you need to choose the perfect bike for you.'" She pointed to the beautiful bike on the page, "What if your mom doesn't have enough money, or you are not allowed? Not everyone can have a bike!"

Anna thought for a second and then said, "Yeah, she's right. My mom told me that I can't get a bike yet because it costs too much and she has to save up."

Michael joined in this new way of thinking more critically, "Right, right, and something else isn't true. You have to 'pump your legs,' but some kids don't have strong legs. Some kids have trouble even walking."

Lauren, watching this seemingly magical moment unfold, understood the group had embarked on some important thinking. She decided to teach them to use their ideas to think both about inclusion and about the impact their thinking could have on the community and the world.

Lauren validated the work the group had done: "Wow, you guys did some important noticing." She then coached them to think about the book in new ways. "We've read this book so many times, and we never really thought about that word *everyone*. Sometimes what we read and what we do sends messages and makes people feel left out." Lauren decided to ask the children, "Can you share your thinking with the whole class today and help us think about what we can do to make sure everyone feels included when we are reading books together?" The group's sharing that day began a whole-class inquiry into thinking about books in terms of inclusion and exclusion around ideas of privilege, power, and ableism (Figure 5.11).

During read-aloud one of the questions often became "Who has the power in this story, and how is the power being used?" Charts were made of books that provoked kids' thinking about inclusion and exclusion with kid-written sticky notes of wonderings, noticings, questions, and ideas. The seeds of this inquiry were planted during play.

Figure 5.11 Building the chart on inclusion/exclusion.

Teacher Takeaway Listen closely and carefully to your children. The ideas they construct during play often soar above their everyday thinking, and you can use those ideas to do even bigger thinking work about all kinds of important concepts.

Curriculum Connections: Collaboration and Negotiation

Group Brain Power

Learning and higher-level thinking will flourish when done collaboratively. In *Tools of the Mind,* Elena Bodrova and Deborah Leong (2007) describe Lev Vygotsky's theory of learning as a social process with a collaborative community playing a central role in cognitive development and making meaning. As we teach kids to collaborate and negotiate in play by listening closely, asking thoughtful questions, and valuing the ideas of others, we are setting them up to strengthen and exponentially deepen their learning across the day and across the curriculum.

Speaking and Listening

Speaking and listening are fundamental to collaboration and negotiation as well as being foundational skills for growing as readers and writers. When kids are talking and listening to others, it deepens their understandings as they ask questions, process what others are saying, discuss topics, and collaborate and negotiate. Good listeners are rare and valued in our culture but essential for true collaboration.

During play, we are teaching kids to really listen by reading body language and facial expressions, offering empathy, and hearing what others have to say without interrupting them. We are also coaching kids in the art of asking thoughtful questions such as, "What are you thinking about this idea? I hear you saying _____, but what about _____? How can we do this together?" The value of speaking and listening reaches into academic and social situations as well as life in general.

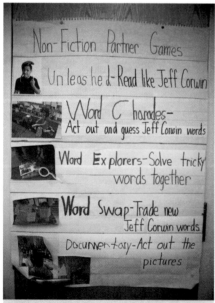

Figure 5.12 Some nonfiction reading-partner games. (See Appendix C for more reading partner games.)

Reading

The power of partnerships! What better way to infuse play into reading workshop than with partnership games (Figure 5.12)? When kids are engaged in partnerships, they have unlimited possibilities to read, think, and talk together with tons of opportunities to explore, play, teach, and collaborate. We recommend that partnerships are formed with two readers who are reading books at similar levels so both partners are able to have active roles in the partnership games.

Writing

Writing partnerships are a powerful structure for children to use collaboration strategies they have learned through play. Writing partners can support each other in a number of ways. Partners might:

- listen to each other, and offer compliments and suggestions.
- ask for help with a particular strategy they are trying.
- read each other's writing, and mark up places that need editing (e.g., circle misspelled sight words and missing punctuation).
- rehearse their writing together.
- decide to coauthor a book.

All these routines require the skills of collaboration. Partners must negotiate how they want their time together to go, and they must use their active listening skills in order to be a supportive partner. When coauthoring a book, partners need to come up with a topic, often compromising their own idea for the betterment of the joint effort. They also need to plan together and determine who will write which part.

Math

Similar to reading, games can be a playful way to increase collaboration and feelings of play. As a matter of fact, math games provide all the benefits of playing games with rules, as described in Chapter 2. Math games can vary from grade level to grade level and in sophistication (Figure 5.13).

Social Studies

Social studies is the study of human life and human stories. As children explore a topic by poring over photographs, reading books and articles, watching videos, and taking multiple field trips, they can pay close attention to the ways they see people collaborating. For example, in a family study, children might notice how each member of the family takes on a different role as they work

Figure 5.13 A teacher helps two students negotiate.

together in the kitchen preparing a meal. These noticings can serve as a launch pad of sorts to classroom conversations about the defining characteristics of collaboration and negotiation and what it looks like in all of its forms.

In play, children are constructing meaning while developing their own rules. Vivian Paley (2005) emphasizes the concepts of collaboration and negotiation by describing the appropriate curriculum for young children as one that includes "fantasy, friendship, and fairness." As children begin to understand and experiment with the principles of collaboration and negotiation, they are writing their own curriculum of friendship and fairness and constructing an understanding of the power of listening and hearing and valuing the perspective of others.

6

PLAY AND A GROWTH MINDSET

It is winter in a second-grade classroom, and three students are trying to build the Queensboro Bridge. They are surrounded by blocks, string, Lego people, and diagrams and photos of the bridge. It is the second time the bridge has fallen, and the budding engineers are trying to figure out what they can do to keep it up this

third time. As they brainstorm ideas, two big things jump out at the casual onlooker. The first is that they are deeply, deeply immersed in this project; the second is that there is no anger or defeat as they contemplate the challenge in front of them.

The students' approach to the failures they have suffered thus far is indicative of something else they possess: a growth mindset. The improvisational nature of play makes it a natural partner to a growth mindset (Brown, 2010, 17). As one is lost in play, problems arise, and improvisation must occur (Figure 6.1). If there are too

Figure 6.1 Getting ready to take a big leap, literally and figuratively.

many kids who want to play Batman, they may become an Avengers super team instead. Flexibility and innovation are rewarded with the sheer pleasure of playing. Play, in its many forms, teaches children what we want them to know about life at large: Failures and frustration happen, but an ability to adapt and improvise often brings unexpected rewards.

Growth Mindset: An Exploration

Carol Dweck, author of *Mindset* (2006), found that most individuals tend to adopt one of two mindsets—a fixed mindset or a growth mindset—or a mixture of both. In a fixed mindset one believes that intelligence is static—either you are smart or you are not. According to Dweck, when individuals adopt this type of mindset they believe things should come easily to them; if they have to apply effort and hard work, they must not be smart. Because of this, these individuals tend to avoid challenges or give up easily when faced with a difficult task. You can probably picture some students in your class who are like this. Maybe they are the students who crumple up their writing papers after not being able to spell a word or exclaim, "I can't do this! I'm not good at math" after trying to solve a challenging problem. Or maybe if you are like us, this reminds you a little bit of yourself in certain aspects of your life.

On the other hand, individuals who have a growth mindset believe that intelligence can be developed and that effort is how one becomes successful (Figure 6.2). These individuals tend to embrace challenges and seek feedback from others. They persist when things get difficult, often showing flexibility in their use of strategies. They are reflective and learn from their mistakes.

Figure 6.2 This child demonstrates something she has been working on for weeks at recess.

But how do children end up with one mindset instead of the other? In their book, *Dispositions* (2014), Arthur Costa and Bena

Kallick refer to growth mindset qualities, such as persistence, flexibility, metacognition, curiosity, and risk-taking, as dispositions. They explored the question, "Are dispositions innate, learned, or both?" What they discovered was very similar to what researchers found with empathy (discussed in Chapter 4). Many of these dispositions are innate and can either grow and develop over time with practice, or they can become stunted if the right conditions are not present (51). For example, babies are born curious. At the youngest age they are fascinated by a light switching on and off and mesmerized by their reflection in a mirror. When they become toddlers they get into everything and try to figure out how things work, and when they begin to talk their favorite question is "why?" By the time they get to school we can see the kids who delight in asking questions and who try to figure things out on their own as opposed to the kids who just want to know the answer.

How does this change happen? According to Costa and Kallick it happens because of a child's environment. For example, when a child's environment is "nonresponsive or barren" and when children are discouraged from asking questions or are not allowed to take risks, the development of certain dispositions can be inhibited (52). The unintentional consequences of praise can also inhibit the development of these dispositions. According to Dweck, praising children for being smart or for learning things quickly and easily can send fixed mindset messages to children. What children hear and begin to believe from these messages is that if things *don't* come quickly and easily to them, they must *not* be smart. Dweck suggests that to encourage a growth mindset we should praise effort and process, rather than praising intelligence and talent. For example, instead of saying, "Wow! You are a math whiz!" one should say, "Wow! You worked so hard on that problem and tried a lot of different strategies to figure it out. Way to go!" In his book, *Punished by Rewards* (1993), Alfie Kohn cited a study that said that children who are motivated by external rewards, such as praise, used less sophisticated strategies to help them learn and scored lower on standardized tests than students who were motivated by the act of learning alone.

New findings in brain research show that the brain has the ability to be rewired throughout our lives and that with effort and practice we can change our brain's functions (Costa and Kallick, 2014). In other words, we have the ability to change our mindset and the dispositions that come along with it. We, of course, believe that the best place to grow and change one's mindset is through play. When children play they are uninhibited and most often not focused on an end product. That same child who crumples his paper during writing time when he doesn't know how to spell a word will surprise you during play by making a sign and inventing a spelling for an unfamiliar word. This is because in play children are not seeking approval from adults, and they know there are no consequences for failure. Gray states, "In the absence of concern about failure and others' judgments, children at play can devote all of their attention to the skills at which they are playing" (2013, 154). A child who might give up easily on a challenging academic task may show persistence when faced with the challenge of the monkey bars. What a child learns in play lays the foundation for learning in other contexts. The question is, how do we get children to recognize and develop their growth mindset during play so it can be transferred to other contexts, and for some children, how do we teach into a growth mindset during play?

Exploring Growth Mindsets in Play

There are few better places for children to understand the relationship between risk and reward than play. From gathering the courage to climb to the top of the play structure, to the feeling of success when finally balancing two blocks just right, play sets a model for living with resiliency and optimism. Not every child comes to school with play experiences that have facilitated the development of a growth mindset, nor, unfortunately, does every child keep that buoyancy throughout their beginning years of school. Because of this, we believe intentional instruction about a growth mindset through play is critical.

As in previous chapters, these sections serve as a tutorial of sorts, helping you think about when to focus on growth mindsets in your classroom, what to teach to help children develop their resilience and persistence, and how to keep this work alive across the day, no matter the subject area. If you see children expressing frustration or boredom in play, or in other, more academic parts of the day, take that as a sign that time should be spent on developing better habits of mind. Refusal, fear, or reluctance can all signal that a child needs support in understanding that failure and frustration are part of their learning, not part of their personhood.

Focus Area: Brains, Like Bodies, Can Grow and Change

The first step in thinking differently about mindset is understanding that the brain is not fixed—it's flexible and can change. Building a growth mindset also means fostering characteristics like optimism, flexibility, resilience, and persistence, which allow a person to develop a positive and growth-minded perspective. To help some children, this may mean capturing a moment of resilience and naming for the child what she did that was so powerful. For other children, this may mean teaching more specific positive self-talk to get through difficulty.

In *A Mindset for Learning* (2015), authors Kristi Mraz and Christine Hertz identify several effective strategies for helping children become more persistent, resilient, empathic, optimistic, and flexible.

- *Storytelling*: The brain remembers in stories, and so telling and retelling stories of when children used these powerful characteristics helps them learn these strategies as a way of approaching challenges in the future.

- *Self-Talk*: Psychologist Ethan Kross has found that "how people conduct their inner monologues has an enormous effect on their success in life" (Weintraub, 2015, 53). Helping children talk their way into challenging situations and out of trouble is one of the best gifts that play can give to children.

- *Reflection*: Looking back over what went well, and what did not, can help children think through ways to approach similar events in the future in the healthiest way possible.

- *Goal Setting*: Having an attainable goal can often help people stick with something through the hard parts. Goals provide purposeful destinations for children and a reason to keep working. For example, "I am Batman, and I need to make a Batman costume."

Each of these strategies can be captured and made explicit during play. Imagine, for example, telling a story about a child who used persistence and resilience to build a tall structure even though it kept falling. A story like this serves as a scaffold for children who do not always think in the most positive ways and a reminder for children who do. See Figures 6.3–6.6.

Possible Teaching Sessions: *Brains, Like Bodies, Can Grow and Change*

When children need support with	You might teach
Talking oneself through challenges	▷ How to talk to yourself when things are hard.  Figure 6.3 The steps for talking to yourself.
Recovering from mistakes	▷ Reflect on what happened, and generate options to make it work better next time. ▷ Use self-talk to calm down and start again.  Figure 6.4 A chart to help children deal productively with mistakes.  Figure 6.5 A chart with questions to help change outcomes

When children need support with	You might teach
Trying something new	▷ Set goals. Ask yourself: What do I want to do/make? Who can help me? ▷ Make a step-by-step plan before you start.

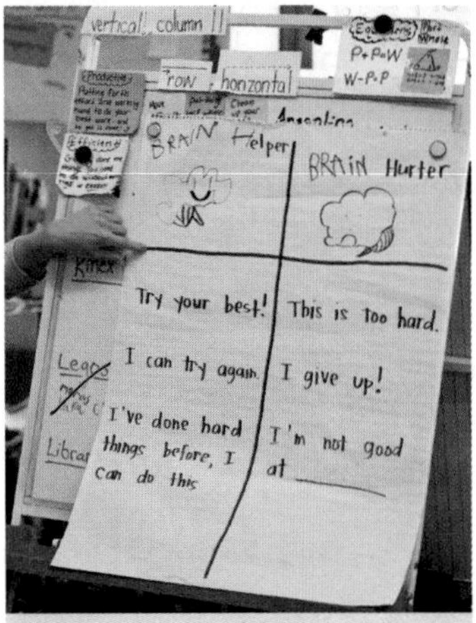

Figure 6.6 Brain Helpers and Brain Hurters (positive self-talk versus negative self talk).

When children need support with	You might teach
Sticking with a challenge	▷ Use self-talk to help you get through this. ▷ Take a break and get back in.

Lesson: When the Going Gets Tough, the Tough Get Talking to Themselves

In this launching session, we teach children a way to talk themselves through challenging or frustrating situations. Psychologist Ethan Kross has found "the more that children self-talk during make believe play, the more likely they are to carry that into adulthood, setting the stage for a lifetime of self-regulation" (Weintraub, 2015, 54). The key to successful self-talk is using your own name, almost as if you are talking to a friend. When you do, you are more likely to be kinder, gentler, more helpful, and less accusatory.

Materials:

- Chart paper to record tips for self-talk
- Blocks or Legos

Procedure (8–10 minutes):

1. Gather the class and introduce the concept. "When something feels hard, we can help ourselves by giving ourselves our very own how-to directions, like we do sometimes when we are trying to tie our shoes. Lots of people call this 'talking to myself.' I am going to try talking to myself through some trouble."

2. Start building with blocks, have them fall, mime frustration, and say, "I am the worst. I can never build with blocks, ever!"

3. Pause and say, "Wait! That's not going to help. I have to give myself my own how-to directions. Watch and see if you can notice exactly what I do."

4. Before building again take a dramatic deep breath and say, "OK, Alison, you can build a tall tower if you go slowly. Now, which block goes on the bottom? Oh, the big one!"

5. Continue to build and narrate, making smarter building choices as you go. "Now let's try this one next. So far so good . . . ooops! It fell again. Let's try putting it the other way and see if that sticks. Oh! Much better!"

6. Ask the class, "What did you notice I did to give myself a how-to?"

7. Listen as children share with partners on the rug, and record what you hear on sticky notes to add to the chart.

8. Wrap up, link to learning, and add in any important points children may not have identified. "Giving yourself some how-to directions is a great way to help yourself do something new or hard. You guys noticed that it helps to:

   ◆ Say your name (not I or me).
   ◆ Take a deep breath.

- ◆ Think before you do it.
- ◆ Say each thing you should do.
- ◆ Use kind words to help yourself.

"When you go off to play today, try something a little hard! Use your how-to directions to help you through it!"

End-of-Play Share Possibilities:

- Have a child replay his self-talk or say how his self-talk helped him through a challenge.

- List helpful self-talk and hurtful self-talk.

- Practice generating helpful self-talk for things like spelling tricky words, solving a math problem, or cleaning up a big mess in blocks (Figure 6.7).

Figure 6.7 Helping a child with his self-talk.

As children develop positive ways of thinking about themselves and about challenge in play, that work can be leveraged into more academic work. This peek into the classroom in second grade demonstrates just how powerful play can be for the rest of the school day.

Peek Inside the Classroom

Storytelling and Inquiry:
Connecting Growth Mindset in Play to Classroom Work

Jennifer Frish brought her second-grade class inside from recess and asked them to sit for their community talk. The students grabbed their last sips of water and quickly assembled into a circle on the rug. Before going outside with the students, Jennifer had asked her class to think about the following questions while playing:

* What am I doing while I play outside that I can also do in the classroom?
* What am I doing well? What is challenging for me?

Jennifer joined the circle with her clipboard in hand and started the conversation. "While you were playing today at recess, I was watching you and taking notes on so many interesting things you were doing." Jennifer leaned into the circle and said quietly, "Can I tell you a story? Class 2-409 was on the roof, and the first thing I heard from Aaron, Isaac, Tate, Khalil, and Carlos was 'Where is the football?' They couldn't find the football. Isaac went inside to try to find it, then he came back and said, 'No football.' So I watched them for a little bit while they were just walking around not sure what to do. But . . ." Jen turned to Aaron and Isaac, who were sitting next to her and gestured for them to continue.

Aaron leaned forward and continued the story, "So we found this round foam block thing, and we thought we could use it as a football, and so we just started playing football."

Jennifer stepped outside of the circle and began coaching students toward making a connection to their classroom work. "Remember I had you thinking about what you were doing when you were playing outside that you could also apply to the classroom? So we get outside and the thing you were most looking forward to was getting your hands on the football, but then there was no football. So there was a problem, and what did you do?"

Tate put his thumb up to indicate he had something to say. "We solved our problem by using something else as a football."

Notice How . . .

* Observations from play can spark community talk.
* The story was told bit by bit.
* The ownership of the story went to the students.

Jennifer looked around to the other students on the rug and said, "Let's think about our classroom. Is there any time when you go through a similar situation in the classroom? Turn and talk with the person next to you, and share your thinking." As the students all began talking, Jennifer moved around the rug to listen in to various groups. She crouched down by Finn and asked him if he could share his thinking with the large group. He nodded, so Jennifer called the students back together, letting them know Finn was going to share his thoughts.

Finn said, "Something similar in the classroom is when we do our math problems." Jennifer asked Finn to explain more, and he responded, "Well, for example, they had no football and then found something to play with, and in a math problem you might not know the answer but then have to figure it out."

"So Finn, are you saying when there is a problem you have to solve it?" Finn nodded. Jennifer turned to Aaron and Isaac. "So thinking about this football issue, what did you have to do to get to the solution? Can you tell the story of what happened?"

Isaac leaned forward on his knees and said, "First we walked out the door and searched by the mini sandbox. We looked all over but couldn't find it, and that made us angry. Then I went inside and tried to look for the football and couldn't find it. Then I went back out and saw this little foam block and threw it. It went really far, and I thought it could be a good football. It worked out really well."

Jennifer smiled, "I am noticing that Isaac tried to do something to solve the problem. He looked for the ball, and when that didn't work, he tried something else. He found something that could be used in place of the football. What does that make you think about the classroom?"

Notice How . . .

* Turn and talks are used to include the entire community.
* Rather than naming the connection for students, Jennifer invites the students to make the connection.

Several students raised a quiet thumb, and Isaac, being the last one to talk, called on Ellie. "Sometimes things can be useful," she said. "You have to try experiments and take risks, and it can work out." Jennifer jotted the words *experiment* and *risks* onto the easel. The discussion continued, and Ellie called on Annabelle.

"I have something to add on. When we measure long things in math, if you don't have a big measurement stick, you can use a little one instead. So it's not that hard—you can always find a solution to some things. You don't always have to get frustrated and give up. Just keep on trying and be persistent."

Jennifer jotted Annabelle's words onto the easel and closed the conversation by saying, "Persistent is a really important word to take away from today. Another big thing that we can walk away with today is that we learn lessons from play. Challenging situations like the football scenario happen every day. We want to pay attention to these things, learn from them, and apply what we learned to the classroom." She then invited the students to turn to their neighbors and share any other lessons they learned from their play that day. Jennifer moved around the rug and added to the chart other lessons she heard students saying.

Notice How . . .

* Students take ownership of the conversation by calling on one another.
* Jotting students' key ideas onto the easel is a way to keep the conversation focused and validate students' ideas.
* The teacher wrapped up the conversation by connecting it to future ongoing work in the classroom.

Social Action: Kids to the Rescue!

When you dream of something, you can begin to take it upon your-self, make it yours, change it. But you have to dream it first.

—Henry Hampton, filmmaker and activist

A growth mindset is essential to social activism. To bring about change, we have to believe things *can* change and not just accept them the way they are. We have to stay focused on what we can do, not on what we can't. In his article "Teaching for Social Justice: One Teacher's Journey" (2007), Bob Peterson talks about five characteristics that are essential for a social activism curriculum.

1. It has roots in the lives of the students.
2. Reflective dialogue is an integral part of the process.
3. There is ongoing questioning and problem posing.
4. There are structures in place to critique bias.
5. There is specific teaching of activism for social justice.

Because of construction work, the play yard of a South Bronx school was closed for several months, meaning no outdoor play for 500 little ones. And while the teachers, principal, and parents worked feverishly to change the situation, with little success, it was the kids of class 2-204 that took action and found a solution.

Saint Mary's Park, directly across from the school, was at one time a lovely urban space with gentle, grassy slopes, tennis and basketball courts, and picnic tables. But due to neglect, Saint Mary's had fallen on hard times and had become a place to avoid in the neighborhood. It was Ephraim who first brought up the topic during morning meeting. As soon as Ephraim suggested the kids could use the park during recess, there was a chorus of objections from the other second graders. The park had always been off limits because it wasn't clean or well tended. Laura, their teacher, realized that this was an ideal opportunity to teach kids how to affect social change.

The inquiry started with group discussions about why the park had been neglected and what they, as a class, could do to make it a place for kids to play. Next, the class shared the book, *The Streets Are Free* (based on a true story) by Kurusa, a story of children in a crowded neighborhood in Caracas, Venezuela, who have no place to play (see Appendix D for other recommended books about social activism). When the kids try to use the streets, they are scolded by adults. Their collective anger and determination leads them to city hall to ask that an abandoned lot be converted to a playground. The children eventually get the lot, and the community works together to make it a safe place for kids to play.

After many class conversations, which included much reflection and lots of questions, ideas, and problem solving, with support from Laura the class decided on a three-pronged approach.

1. They would write letters to the mayor and parks department about taking better care of the park. They would use the strategies they learned in a persuasive writing unit to convince the recipients to act.
2. They would mobilize other kids in the school and their families to write letters and emails.
3. They would ask the parents' association to buy them large garbage bags and disposable gloves and go to the park every day for twenty minutes to pick up rubbish.

At first, they received little attention and no response to their letters. And still, every day they would go over to Saint Mary's to work together to make the park cleaner. When they felt particularly discouraged about their lack of progress, they would reread *The Streets Are Free* and talk about the persistence and resilience of the children of Caracas and how they could do the same.

The kids of class 2-204 began to see firsthand that persistence matters. As they mobilized and took action, their families began to see the importance of this issue to them and what they were doing to help the community. Their passion for the project spread. The parks department did eventually respond to the barrage of correspondence and began to send crews to clean and maintain the grounds and empty the trash. The children and families, finally able to use the park for recess, experienced the true power of a growth mindset.

Teacher Takeaway Social activism is powerful and effective when grounded in students' lives. Take issues in kids' lives that matter, and with questioning, problem solving, and reflective conversations, help them to see that with a growth mindset they have power to impact change.

Curriculum Connections: Growth Mindset

The Promise of Yet: Thinkers Grow in Reading, Writing, Math, and the Content Areas

Reading

One of the important components of the reading workshop is the share and reflection time at the end. Children's work is highlighted as they share it with the group. Often we select work to share because it meets the standard of what all students are

Figure 6.8 A chart, made by teacher Katie Lee, helps students select how they want to share.

expected to achieve. We can reframe the share session to celebrate growth mindset thinking. For example, suppose you have a reader who has been chosen to share based on his strong work in making his voice match the character's feelings. Rather than simply having him share this skill, have him share the process that brought him to read this way (Figure 6.8). "I used to read the words on the page and not think about the character, but now I think about how the character is feeling and make my voice sound that way." Perhaps he could model how he used to read in a flat tone and how he is reading expressively now.

Writing

Writing is a natural place to celebrate a growth mindset (Figure 6.9). Similar to reading work, rather than celebrating published pieces of writing alone, we can have mini-celebrations across the unit of study to highlight the process of writing. We can share how the stories we told became written words, and how those words were revised and edited to bring our stories to life. We can have a place in our classrooms to hang up drafts of writing, and we can highlight and label places where students

Figure 6.9 A student reflects on how her brain grew as a writer.

used a growth mindset. For example, "Joseph was persistent when he tried to spell the word three different ways!" When we do celebrate our published pieces, we can have students reflect on their process and what they learned that helped them to become stronger writers in this unit of study.

Math

As children encounter challenges in math, we can have them reflect on what they did when they were faced with a challenge. Did they ask for help? Give up? Try one strategy, then try another? Once children identify their learning behaviors, we can name the important dispositions behind them—persistence, flexibility, metacognition—and note whether they indicate a growth or fixed mindset. Children can set goals for themselves in these areas and reflect on them periodically, considering how a growth mindset is helping them become better learners of mathematics.

Social Studies

Social studies gives kids opportunities to make sense of what they are noticing, wondering, and thinking about in the world around them. If we are alert as teachers, we will see that the dispositions of a growth mindset are defining themes in many of the human stories that unfold around us. For example, a group of first graders engaged in a neighborhood study were observing and taking notes on a high-rise construction project adjacent to their school. As the children watched, a crane hoisted a load of materials, but the wind kept preventing it from placing the materials where they were supposed to be. The first graders noticed how the construction workers kept trying and ultimately placed the materials in their designated spot. Later that day at meeting, Tara (the teacher) coached the children to connect what was happening at the construction site to the ideas of perseverance and resilience. The children had seen the workers doing exactly what they were learning to do in play and across the day to make their work stronger. Social studies is at its best when it transcends facts and information and grows into concepts and ideas.

Assessment

At the time of this writing, we are working in an era of accountability and standards in teaching. Oftentimes the spotlight settles solely on products and outcomes, and the learner can, unfortunately, be lost. As educators, we cannot let that happen! We want our classrooms to be places where kids can think, talk, read, write, and play, and where products are the outcomes of a developing process.

If we truly believe a growth mindset is vital for children's positive growth and development, then we can't just teach about it, we also have to assess children across the curriculum with their growth in mind. Assessment conversations that look at growth in learning are very different from those that look only at finished products. In New York City, as in many school districts across the country, students are generally evaluated within a fixed framework as level 1, 2, 3, and 4. A child who hasn't met the grade-level benchmark in reading, for example, would be a level 1 or 2. The issue with such a system is that a level 1 or 2 can be seen as a failure, discreet and different from levels 3 or 4, as opposed to just a point on a learning progression. A child on the receiving end of a level 1 may see herself as "not smart" or a failure.

Now let's think about this same child through the lens of a growth mindset. While she may not have met the grade-level benchmark in reading, if she is assessed on a continuum that includes "not yet" instead of a grade or numerical rating that indicates failure, there is a sense of hope. A child can move along the continuum, and we as teachers can help her get there with helpful strategies and support. It's a whole different way of seeing the child, and it suggests that, even if she's not there yet, she most certainly will be in the future.

Watch young children at play, and you will see that there are few opportunities for "failure" but many opportunities to problem solve creatively, perhaps branching off in new directions, or buckling down to understand the root of the toppling block tower and addressing it. If we do our job well as teachers, children transfer this play mindset into their lives at large: when solving math problems, tackling difficult passages in reading, or rebounding from a conflict with a friend in the cafeteria. The true gift of a growth mindset, and one of the many gifts of play, is the understanding that there is no challenge that does not also come with the gift of possibility.

enraged

angry

annoyed

discouraged

frustrated

mad

bossy

A volcano created in the art center becomes a source of new vocabulary.

Section III
The Play in Work
The Whole Day Can Feel Playful

Play is our brain's favorite way of learning.
—Diane Ackerman

Up until this point, we have written about play in its most generally accepted forms: running, jumping, building, drawing, and pretending. But what about the rest of the day? Reading, writing, math? Certainly all of those things happen within the context of play, but what about the standalone, content-area time during the day? Children don't stop being children when choice time is over and recess has finished. The element of play and joy can, and should, be the interconnecting thread of all you do in the classroom. There is no reason for a "play is over, time for work" mentality. We believe there is play in work and work in play. It helps, however, to have practical ways to carry that mindset into all aspects of the curriculum. From your environment and materials, to your language, to your approach to lessons, you can infuse the core elements of joy and engagement that make learning through play so effective. In the following chapters, we explore the possibility that the whole day can feel like play.

As you read on, hold tight to the idea that no matter what curriculum you are asked to teach, you have the power to make it playful and joyful. There is no "they" that can stop you from finding the lightness and pleasure of learning.

Two boys enjoy a Star Wars story.

7

THE POWER OF TAPPING INTO STUDENT INTERESTS

When Adele Schroeter and Alison Porcelli, principal and vice principal of a New York City Public School, walk the halls on the day before school starts, they are looking for blank spaces. Adele and Alison look for empty bulletin boards, materials waiting to be labeled, and uncluttered shelves. When they find such spaces, they are content. They know that only when teachers have made the space open for children to fill with their own unique passions and dreams that the classrooms and the school are ready for kids to enter. A school like theirs is a blank canvas waiting for the bright vibrant strokes of children to make their mark upon it (Figure 7.1).

A classroom environment filled to the brim with the personality of the teacher leaves little room for the interests and growing passions of each child. We, as teachers, have our homes to fill up with the posters and trinkets we love, but our classrooms are our children's to design and develop. The same is true for

Figure 7.1 Two girls work industriously to decorate their classroom.

our curriculum. We are not teaching "students"; we are teaching Paloma, and Sammie, and DeAndre, and Alex, each with a unique viewpoint and access point to the world. When we connect to each student, truly and personally, we build the relationships essential to teaching and learning.

Learning what makes our students tick, from their styles of learning, to their loves and pet peeves, enables us to tailor curriculum in ways big and small. When we are able to use students' interests to drive our instruction, we keep learning playful and engaging. Why should that matter? It matters because engaged and joyful learners become engaging and joyful people in the world around them. It matters because how we teach is as important as what we teach. It matters that we acknowledge what our children love because through that we acknowledge that they count, that they are valued, and that they are valuable. It matters because our children matter.

Incorporating student interests in our instruction is also one of the simplest and most accessible ways to achieve a play mindset while, ostensibly, doing "work" (Figure 7.2). The deep engagement children achieve while playing "store" can be accessed and leveraged throughout a whole day of learning. This chapter will help you identify and use student interests to find the play in work.

Figure 7.2 This reading chart celebrates a love of superheroes in the classroom.

Student Interests: An Exploration

There is an idea, pervasive in popular movies and TV shows, that school is boring. A fun teacher, a good day, or an engaging class is remembered as an anomaly and not the norm. Even worse, to our minds, is that the idea of school as boring or grueling is accepted and even considered necessary by some. Playful, engaging classrooms do not preclude students from learning about hard work; in fact, during play, children are often working harder than they are when asked to perform academic tasks (Figure 7.3). Or as Dr. Spock puts it, "A child loves his play, not because it's easy,

Figure 7.3 This complicated and ornate block structure shows evidence of planning, revision, and stamina and is more than just "cute."

Figure 7.4 Listening closely to children is an essential skill for teachers.

but because it's hard." Invoking a spirit of play and utilizing children's interests put us in the advantageous position of better understanding our students, while giving them the space to be curious and improvisational.

Getting to know the children in your classroom, their interests, their passions, and their pet peeves has powerful and long-lasting benefits for children (Figure 7.4). In their book *Visible Learning and the Science of How We Learn* (2014), John Hattie and Gregory Yates write, "Establishing positive relationships between young students and their teachers has been shown to cascade and so result in lasting benefits involving trust and affection" (17). They've found that positive relationships with teachers have benefits for children *years* down the line. As teachers, we have the power to aid or disrupt the social and emotional development of our small charges.

Establishing these positive relationships has a great deal to do with overcoming natural empathy gaps, which Hattie and Yates define as "when people are relatively unable to put themselves in the place of another person" (16). It can be difficult to think of school from the perspective of a young child when you are swamped with what you need to do as a teacher. When people dismiss play as a waste of time, they are thinking of it from a perspective other than that of the child. When people see the work of children as "cute," they undermine the intense and real effort it took the child to bring that vision to creation. Using children's interests as a springboard to your teaching can help you close the gap between an adult's perspective and a child's perspective.

Just as important, when we bring children's personalities into the classroom, we send the message that they belong in this space. Few things are more powerful than that feeling. In fact, according to Hattie and Yates, "Close and supportive relationships with teachers have the potential to mitigate the risk of negative outcomes for children who may otherwise have difficulty adjusting and succeeding in school" (18–19). That is to say, teachers who create caring relationships with children make a tremendous difference in those children's lives.

How Do I Gather Data on Student Interests?

Sigh *Data*, the dreaded "d" word. From data collection to data entry, has there ever been a more joyless word in the history of education? But what if data meant more than just reading levels or scores on math assessments? What if the data we collected had to do with what our children love and dream about? What if our data was used to create play and engagement in the classroom? Knowing that half the class is holding a pretty deep ninja obsession is *as important* as knowing that 45 percent are below grade level in reading. Want to help move those readers? Now you know part of the equation: Get books about ninjas! When we know what children love, we can use it in our classrooms to make them more joyful, meaningful, and engaging.

When we know the joys our students find in play and imaginary worlds, it helps us see our students first and foremost as *players*. If you know pirates are popular with your students, you can affect a silly pirate accent to send children off to math, and in doing so, you are helping children achieve a play state (Figure 7.5). "Getting oneself in a play state," writes Stuart Brown, "masks the urgent purposefulness and associated anxiety of work, increasing efficiency and productivity" (2010, 133–134). When the teacher blurs the lines between work and play, children are able to access the improvisational potential of play within whatever work they are doing. Brown states it thusly, "There is a great deal of evidence that the road to mastery of any subject is guided by play" (141). When children feel free enough to play at their work, they are more likely to achieve high levels of success. Incorporating student interests and passions is just one way to make that success possible.

Figure 7.5 A classroom post office provides a playful avenue for writing.

Have you ever sat through a professional development workshop, totally and completely bored? Do you remember anything from the workshop besides that feeling? Now, think of a time when that was not the case, when you perked up, leaned forward, and started scribbling notes at a furious pace—in short, when you became interested. Did the topic shift to one you cared about? Did you identify with the speaker and feel heard? The interests of an educator at a professional conference may be different from the interests of the four-year-old squirming on the rug, but the feeling is the same: the feeling of being seen and spoken to, the feeling of engagement and passion, the feeling of "finally, yes, this is what I have been waiting for!" For the four-year-old this may be the chance to get the mail; for the six-year-old it could be the reference to My Little Pony; for the eight-year-old, an analogy to quidditch. This is the feeling of play meeting work, and we can bring this feeling into our classrooms when we get to know our students' interests.

Early in the year, we recommend a close and careful study of your students' likes and dislikes. You can employ several ways to gather intel on children's private passions, and each one offers different potentials for understanding what children truly and deeply care about. You learn very different things, for example, when you talk to children instead of just observing them. A child may wear Super Mario shirts and you presume he's a fan, only to find out his true passion is something as obscure as vacuum cleaners (true story).

For the purpose of this chapter, we are categorizing student interests as both topics the child cares about and a child's preferred way of learning about the world—doing, reading, talking. The two are nearly inseparable, as even the most interesting topics can be made uninteresting through unceasing lecture.

Observation

Observation is one of the main ways that we, as people, make theories about other people. We see someone in a shirt with a band on it, and we assume they enjoy music. We see someone cooing to a baby, and we assume they love all children. Observation without conversation can be dangerous; sometimes the shirt is a gift, sometimes we love our own nieces and barely tolerate other babies. The same is true with children. Though some may pick out their clothes and their backpacks, others may be wearing hand-me-downs.

We can learn about our children in every corner of the day, from where they sit when they want a moment's peace to the books they hang on to week after week. Yet first we have to become kid-conscious, aware that every action and choice they make gives us valuable information about who they are. We must push our worries about what's next aside and fully appreciate and learn about the children we see now. Only when we are fully present with children can we truly close the empathy gap and teach them to the fullest of our ability. Too often we dismiss things as unimportant (love of ninjas) because we believe we have truly important things on our minds (reading levels). But if it is important to a child, we must make it important to ourselves because we will help children along our agenda only if we honor theirs as powerful and meaningful in its own right.

Questions to Consider When Observing for Children's Interests:

- When given free time to draw, what objects or scenes does the child draw?
- When given free choice to write, what topics does the child write about?
- When given free range of the library, what books does the child settle with?
- What are the child's most common play themes in free play?
- What does the child talk about with her peers during unstructured times?
- When given free choice, what is a child most drawn to: running around, talking with friends, or drawing?
- What tasks does the child seem most engaged in? Least engaged in?
- Does the child prefer large groups? Small? To be on his own?
- What part of the room is the child most drawn to? The rug? The tables?
- What materials is the child most drawn to? What about during recess?

If you record these observations you will see that they are invaluable in helping you understand the whole child (see Appendix E for a Student Interest Recording Sheet). For example, a child may appear not to like math, but the real issue is that sitting at a table is not a good match for her physicality. A simple switch to the floor begets different math results. Or a different child may seem not to understand a story when he writes about it, but when he draws a summary, his understanding shows an incredible depth. Small, simple changes like this can make big differences for children. When you observe children closely, you'll know them more completely and be better able to help them reach their full potential.

Figure 7.6 A love of soccer has driven this child's reading, writing, and playing life for an entire year.

Conversations

"Would you please tell me about your picture?" Kindergarten teachers probably ask this question more than any other in the first weeks of school. The question helps us assess a myriad of academic skills (representational drawing, oral language development, fine motor development) and also fall in love with the personalities of each and every child. With that question, Aqil's blue and black tornado actually turns out to be Dr. Who's Tardis. Henry's daily explosions of red and repetition of the letters JPL are his rockets, labeled for the NASA Jet Propulsion Lab, and Elles has a parade of ponies who are heading off to the pony parade. The conversations this question sparks are key to understanding children's interests and passions—passions as vital to their core as your love of cooking (Figure 7.6).

The beginning of school can feel like a rush to assess and assess and assess. And yes, it is important to find the many strengths that children bring to school, but it is equally important to build a personal connection with each and every child because those connections will ultimately make our classrooms successful. Finding time to get to know children can seem daunting in the beginning of school, so we suggest a few simple tips to help you get to know the whole child.

- Divide your conference notes into two columns: one side for typical assessment data, and the other for notes about children's interests, passions, and preferred activities.

- While observing more traditional academics, ask questions about students' interests. For example, "What do you love to write about?" tackles both interests and generating strategies for writing (see Appendix F for additional questions that can help you learn more about your children) (Figure 7.7).

- Keep a checklist of who you have had face-to-face interactions with so you will notice the kids who may slip quietly into the background.

- Incorporate morning shares or show and tell. As children develop their oral language and conversational skills, you will learn about the passions and interests of each child.

Figure 7.7 Whole-class conversations are a great time to learn more about your students.

It's important to remember that relationships require constant maintenance, and children change rapidly. Olav, who first played only Star Wars at recess, shifted to Ninjas and never looked back. Getting to really know someone can be a lifelong affair, and as teachers, we honor that by taking time for conversations with children all year, not just in the early "get-to-know-you" rush. The key, of course, is to gather data routinely and then use it to transform your classroom into a world where all work has an element of play.

How Do I Use Student Interests?

As teachers, we create the environment that invites children to deeply engage with their learning. If we bring children books about topics they love, they bring the enthusiasm to work on the strategies that help them read those books (Figure 7.8). Work doesn't have to be unpleasant. Children gathered around the Marvel characters compendium are stretching just as many words, making

Figure 7.8 A spooky books basket in the classroom library.

just as much meaning, and arguably engaging more than the child reading Lesson 7 out of the reading anthology. Of course, this is not a book about teaching reading (see Appendix G for a list of book titles that do that topic justice). This is a book about infusing a mindset of play and joy throughout the day, while still meeting benchmarks along the way. Now that you know what children love, we suggest you can use it powerfully to do just that.

Adapting Classroom Libraries

Look at the labels of your book baskets—do they look like they've been organized with the children in mind? Do the topics in your library match your children's interests? Do you analyze the library this way throughout the year? If no, there are myriad ways to add books, beyond going personally bankrupt.

- Have your school buy books! Companies that cater to schools, like Book Source, Scholastic, or Pioneer Valley Books, can compile book sets based on interest and are often approved sites for school spending. In many schools principals need to spend the money in their budget—usually in the fall or spring—or they will lose it. Many principals ask staff if they need anything; however, most of us are so busy at that point in the year that we miss the opportunity. Our advice is to get ahead of the game. Because it happens every year, create a running list of books that match students' interests. Then, when your principal puts out the invitation, you are ready to accept!

- Use your local library! Many libraries have partnerships with school districts that allow teachers to take out unlimited or very high quantities of books. That *Frozen* obsession may not last all year, but while your children have it, you can check out books about the characters.

- Make books! If a book does not exist, or if it is inaccessible for a child, make it. Take photos or use approved images from the Internet, and cowrite the text with interested children. These books often become the most popular in the classroom library, like the one shown in Figure 7.9 featuring children from the class and the things they see.

Aasiy   said   "look   at   the rabbit."

Figure 7.9 A page from the class *Look at It!* book.

■ Think nontraditional! Teacher and author Kristin Ziemke uses high-interest brochures in her classroom library. Her advice is to stock up in airports: water parks, zoos, ghost tours! All free to take, and all very popular with children.

A Note About Book Choice and Levels and Libraries

There are many, many opinions about the best way to help children learn how to read. We believe the best way involves choice, engagement, and thoughtful instruction. To that end, we advocate for a well-organized, thoughtfully selected classroom library that has both unleveled and leveled books, all of high interest to children. How the library is organized depends on what works best for you and your children. We have seen successful libraries organized by topics with mixed levels in each basket, and we have seen libraries with a section organized by level and a section organized by topic, with children shopping in each section. We have seen libraries with no levels but careful, thoughtful instruction about choosing a book that feels just right, knowing that there are many ways a book can be "just right." What's most important is that the library reflects your children and supports their growth as readers.

Adapting Provided Materials

Many curricula come with materials—alphabet charts, math manipulatives, read-alouds—but there is no reason a classroom must use every material provided, if a replacement material serves the purpose. Company-created material is often made to serve a generic group of children. Ask yourself, "Can I teach the skill or strategy with different content?" Use the material provided as a mentor to craft your own. Alphabet charts, for example, can be swapped out for ones created by students based on their own interests and worldviews (Figure 7.10). There is no reason why "D" must stand for "Dog" when you know from your data that "Darth Vader" is infinitely more engaging to the classroom community.

Likewise, traditional math manipulatives can sit alongside things like stones or beautiful shells that engage children differently and are connected to students'

Figure 7.10 A class-created alphabet chart.

Figure 7.11 Reading a class-adapted book—the pictures are the same, but the words were changed by the class.

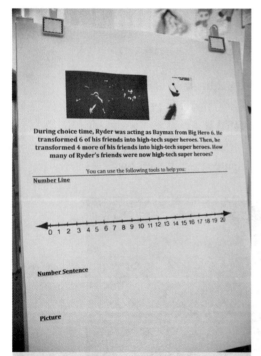

Figure 7.12 Working on a story problem that uses students' names.

interests. Letter writing can be practiced in shaving cream, writing paper can be photocopied in pink, and pens can be silver. The shared reading book for the week can be an adapted class book about letters where students can practice using first letters and the picture to figure out the covered words.

But . . . but . . . but . . . is it still learning? If you know from your data that your most reluctant writer's favorite color is pink, and you photocopy her writing paper on pink so that she wants to write line after line, there is far more learning there than what comes from her staring at white paper. And in the case of this particular writer, after two weeks of pink paper, she had overcome her fear enough that she took the white paper the next week and for the rest of her year. The skills we seek to teach should be transferrable enough, and we should be skilled practitioners enough, that the color of the paper or the topic of the story problem should matter to us only in so much that they are engaging and joyful for children.

Consider, as first-grade teachers Kat and Lizzie did, that to engage children in successful math strategies, you can swap out the story problem in the math book with one that uses names from the class and events that children know (Figures 7.11 and 7.12).

Adapting materials to better reflect your children's passions can be an as-needed approach. When it makes sense for your children, it can be a powerful tool. When it is unneeded, it becomes busywork for the teacher. Ask yourself, "Are my children engaged enough in the content using these materials?" If yes, carry on! If no, adapting or changing materials can be a way to open a door to learning for a child or group of children.

Finding More Choice for Children

Sometimes the simplest way to use student interests is not to create more but to do less. Most often this comes up with choices. If you think about it, children navigate all sorts of choices—all on their own—when they play. Consider the things you dictate to children, and then ask yourself, "How can I empower students to make more of their own choices at other times of the day?" Some choices we have opened to children are:

- Seat: floor, table, bean bag, standing table, single spot, with a group
- Writing utensil: pen, skinny marker, pencil, colored pencil
- Group size: work alone, with a partner, with a group
- Topic in writing
- Book in reading

You may find that you need to teach into the idea of making smart choices, but we believe this is valuable instruction akin to the "give a man a fish" saying. If we forever make choices for children, they do not have opportunities to learn how to make choices, and that can have long-term consequences. Thoughtful decision making is a worthwhile skill to teach.

You may also decide to rearrange your room after getting to know your students (Figure 7.13). If you find many students love to work on the floor, you might move a table to make room for another comfy, cozy rug. In Alison's kindergarten classroom of twenty-six children, she did not

Figure 7.13 A low table creates a space for work and play.

have twenty-six chairs at twenty-six table spots. She had a myriad of seating options designed for the needs and interests of the class.

When children play as mommies, daddies, and teachers, they relish giving orders and making declarations. They have a chance to play with real power. Opening up your classroom so children have chances to make decisions with real consequences gives them another chance to take on the mantle of power and responsibility. Each time they do, children become more confident in their agency and more responsible in their choosing. There are few places where children can pretend to be the adults they will become; school should be one of them.

Teacher Mindset and Language

One of the surest ways to invoke a play mindset in your students, even during the trickiest of work, is to have one yourself. Singing silly transition songs, taking dance breaks, and telling jokes will lighten the feel every day (Figure 7.14). If you have fun, chances are your children will as well. If you share your love for topics, children will as well. In playing with children, we let them see more of who we are, and they grow to know us as we grow to know them. We may be the first to show children the joy of a silly dance, and we may strike a deep chord in them when we share what we love about My Little Pony. When you understand your students' passions, you'll know better how to connect with them and infuse a sense of joy into all you do. One year a third-grade teacher, Christine, had quite a few boys and girls that loved Star Wars, so her transition music was the theme from the movie. The next year it was "Let It Go," alternating with "Everything Is Awesome."

Figure 7.14 Incorporating a dance break.

Knowing your student interests can help you plan lessons that incorporate those interests in meaningful ways. You can show a video clip of Spider Man learning to use his web shooters to illustrate persistence, or draw an analogy to a doctor check-up when teaching about editing your writing. The key to teaching children is remembering what it was like to be one. When planning instruction, you can ask yourself:

- Can I make an analogy to something I know my class enjoys?

- Can I use a visual or story from a topic my class enjoys?

- Is there a prop, a tool, or a movement I can use to make this more engaging?

- Is there a way to incorporate the materials I know my children enjoy using?

Jung Choe, a first-grade teacher, found a simple way to transform her end of writing feedback shares by mimicking her children's favorite TV show: *The Voice* (Figure 7.15). The purpose was the same as it ever was—to be reflective about writing, to receive and give feedback, and to grow as writers through shared study. The method, play-acting as though it were a television show, was revolutionary for the children. When the students stepped into the shoes of Adam Levine (including an arm tattoo made out of paper!), suddenly their advice to each other became honest and specific. Rather than saying, "I liked your poem, it was good," they started saying things like, "Your details really gave me a strong feeling at the beginning. I wonder if you could do more of that?" Playing *The Voice* gave the students a specific vision of feedback based on their experience with the show, and it helped them transfer something they knew from a familiar, playful context to an academic one. Engagement and enthusiasm pervaded the shares, and the writing workshop flourished because of it.

Figure 7.15 *The Voice* share in first grade.

To be clear, we are not suggesting each time you teach that it become a Broadway show; however, humor, songs, ample movement, and references to the topics your children love will infuse more joy and lightness into the day.

Peek into the Classroom: Using Student Interest to Drive Instruction

Third-grade teacher Christine has gathered her mathematicians on the rug in front of the Smartboard. She has cued the clip from the *Empire Strikes Back* where Luke, after a lot of hemming and hawing and fear, finally raises his X-wing from the swamp under Yoda's watchful guidance. She knows many of her students have seen and love this movie. She also knows that her students have been daunted by some of their tricky new math work, so she is taking this opportunity to infuse some playful reflection.

She starts off by saying, "Friends, we are going to watch a clip from *The Empire Strikes Back* a few times. The first time we are just going to watch and enjoy it, and the second time we are really going to try to figure out what is going on with Luke and if that can help us at all in our lives." As she starts the clip, there is a murmur of excitement and then rapt attention for the duration of the three minutes. When it ends, Christine has the children turn and talk, with no specific prompt or question beyond, "What do you think?"

Notice How . . .

- The intention is set up clearly in the beginning.
- The teacher first lets the children respond organically to the clip.
- The clip is short enough to show multiple times.
- The teacher is using her knowledge of both her children's interests and academic needs.

As Christine is about to start the clip for the second time, she gives a "listen for" prompt, saying, "Friends, listen for Luke's self-talk in the clip and what that says about him right in this moment. If you want to jot down or draw a few thoughts, you can. Otherwise, just hold them in your mind till I hit pause again."

Notice How . . .

- The teacher is using some of the growth mindset work from play in this setting.
- There is character work that mirrors work done in reading.
- There are multiple modes of response based on children's preference: drawing, jotting, thinking.

Christine hits pause after Luke's repeated cries of "I can't. It's too big" and gives the children a chance to respond. Most have identified that this attitude is certainly negative. Ryan gestures to the class chart of "brain helpers and brain hurters" and says, "That's the kind of attitude that makes you give up and stop growing."

Christine gathers the class back and then directs them again. "Now listen for how Yoda coaches Luke to a different kind of thinking." Christine starts the clip again, hitting pause right after Yoda chastises Luke saying, "So certain are you." She asks the children to turn and talk again, analyzing Yoda's speech and its impact on Luke.

Notice How . . .

* The teacher treats the clip as worthwhile as any other academic material.
* The thinking skills and talking skills are academic in nature, though the content is from pop culture.
* The children rely on the work they have done through play as a touchstone for thinking about Luke's experience.

The children share out, noticing that Yoda gave some tips about the Force, and even some concrete examples of what to do to manage the Force.

Christine then angles the conversation in the direction she has been heading the whole time, asking, "What do you think the Force is in our world?"

This question has children stumped, some thinking its the air around them, others shrugging.

Christine tries rephrasing and clarifying, asking, "The Force seems to be something that helps you do things, lots of different things, lift ships out of the water, but also influence people and your own body. Is there anything in us we've talked about like that?"

Maya has a moment of inspiration and shouts out, "Your brain!"

There are shouts of agreement, and Christine asks the children to tell their neighbors some examples of how using your brain can be like using the Force. Children volunteer ideas like focusing to get something done, practicing handstands again and again until you can do it, and visualizing before you do something. More concrete examples abound, too—your brain can make your arm lift things up, for example.

Christine now suggests a playful way to approach problems. "Maybe," she says, "when we come to hard things, it might be fun to support each other by reminding each other that we can use the Force. We can become Yodas to each other." Christine tries out Yoda-speak: "Solve hard math problems, can we." The class laughs along with Christine, and a few children try out the Yoda-speak.

"Use a pen, you can."

"Carry the ones, you can."

"Read hard books, you will."

Christine transitions the conversation one more time toward math saying, "Listen, we have some challenging work we are doing in math, but no more challenging than what Luke had to face. Let's think of some Yoda-speak we can use to help our math partners use the Force when it gets hard."

Notice How . . .

* The teacher coached children to transfer the big ideas; it did not happen magically or effortlessly.
* The children are all engaged by talking with each other, and multiple entry points to the conversation can occur.
* The teacher has transitioned into math instruction (naming strategies) but in a playful engaging way.

Figure 7.16 A child brings her joy into the classroom.

Not every child's life is filled with play and joy; sadly, there are many children for whom life is unreliable and scary. All children need spaces safe for laughter and silliness, risk and resilience, and school can be that place. Preparation for the world does not mean preparing children for the worst. It means giving children the best, so that they, in turn, can create a more beautiful world (Figure 7.16). The best for children is honoring their passions and interests and finding ways to incorporate them across the day. The best for children is understanding that movement, song, and opportunities to wiggle are essential to growth. The best for children is to use our pedagogical skill, not to blindly follow curriculum but to create spaces and instruction that say, "You are valued." A sense of play makes schools stronger, and incorporating student interests is the first step in creating it.

8

LIGHTHEARTED TEACHING

Supporting Meaningful Goals with Playful Tools and Charts

In a corner of the rug, Gracie, a first grader clad head to toe in superhero gear, reclines with her baggie of reading books in a bean bag. To the observer from the door, she appears to be poking at her wrist while making "bwyou-bwyou" noises periodically, possibly off task, definitely play-ing. However, the closer one gets, the easier it is to see that she is actually perfectly on task. The poking at her wrist? She is activating various "powers" on her wristband (Figure 8.1), a tool she made with her teacher to help her when she gets stuck, and the "bwyou" noises? They indi-cate she has just "blasted" another hard word.

When did the line between work and play get drawn in school?

Why did the line between work and play get drawn in school?

The idea that play and work stand in oppo-sition is a fallacy. "[T]he opposite of play is not

Figure 8.1 Gracie's blaster bracelet.

work," writes Stuart Brown. "The opposite of play is depression" (2010, 126). Brown argues that "Play is a *state of mind*, rather than an activity" (60). The goals of schooling may not immediately seem playful, but the way we help children get there can. As a child, Kristi hated brushing her teeth, an activity very few would describe as playful. One day, she started talking to her teeth in her head as she brushed. "Time to scrub your back. Ooh boy, that tickles doesn't it?" Each tooth gained a personality over time, until brushing her teeth became fantasy play, a habit that she (somewhat embarrassingly) admits still happens today. The line between work and play is more in one's attitude than one's actual activity. If we demarcate play from work, we teach children to do the same, denying them a chance to see all learning as an opportunity to improvise and innovate.

Sometimes the thing that helps a child achieve a playful state of mind during an admittedly nonplayful task is a tool or chart. Like a block that encourages imaginative sword play, a blaster bracelet can invite a sense of lightness and joy into the sometimes hard work of reading. Which begs the question: Is work done with a sense of play any less meaningful to the learner? We argue no, and in some ways it is the sense of play that brings the meaning for children. Designing playful supports requires an understanding of why we make tools and charts, how goals support children, and how to subsume our own ideas of what "work" looks like for what children really need to be successful, independent, and joyful.

Goals, Tools, and Charts: An Exploration

Have you ever thought you taught something, only to realize you are the only one to remember it? Have you had lessons seem too easy, and everyone is bored, or too hard, and everyone is disengaged? We have, and it's taught us that sometimes the reason something doesn't stick is because it wasn't the right thing to teach to begin with.

Vygotsky (1978) defined the zone of proximal development (ZPD) as "the distance between the actual developmental level as determined by independent problem solving and the level of potential development as determined through problem solving under adult guidance or in collaboration with more capable peers" (83). He went on to explain that the ZPD is something the child might need support with today but will be able to accomplish on her own tomorrow. Jerome Bruner (1978) used the metaphor of scaffolding to describe this type of support: something temporarily in place until the child becomes independent with the instructional goal. While Vygotsky and Bruner suggested that potential development can be reached with adult or peer guidance, providing children with tools or artifacts from instruction can serve as a reminder of the instruction and as a bridge to independence. In other words, tools are

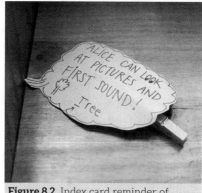

Figure 8.2 Index card reminder of teaching.

a way to help children achieve their goals. For example, after a conference, many teachers leave students with a sticky note or index card (Figure 8.2) with a written reminder of the teaching goal.

While the sticky note does not take the place of the instruction, it helps children remember to continue practicing their goal until they have internalized it. The key here, of course, is to make sure our learners are invested in their goals so they are motivated to carry on independently. Brian Cambourne, author of *The Whole Story* (1993), said that in order for learners to engage with a task, they must be able to see what is in it for them. The task must be meaningful to the child, not something simply assigned by an adult. When thinking about how to cultivate children's true investment in goals and instruction, what better place is there to look than play?

Make Sure the Goals Match the Child

The zone of proximal development is a zone where children are so invested in their work or play that they operate at the outer edge of their potential where, with support, they often accomplish things they didn't know were possible. Marie Clay (1993), founder of Reading Recovery, discussed the importance of building on children's strengths and using a child's errors as a window into a learner's ZPD. An error shows what a child is approximating or trying to do. When we see these errors, it is a clue that the child would benefit from instruction in a particular area. The key is to understand each child's ZPD and to select academic goals for the child with it in mind. Where is this child's energy and investment at this time? What is she already trying to do? What support would help her do it?

Make Goals with, Not for, the Child

Another key aspect of play is that it is self-driven and filled with choice. If you want to get learners to invest in academic goals, give them some choice and control. According to Robert Marzano and Debra Pickering, "Students are more likely to engage in school goals that are linked to their personal goals" (2011, 13). One way a teacher can tap into a learner's personal goals is to give a student a menu of possible goals based on assessment and allow the student to choose which one she wants to work on. This method increases motivation and gives the child a sense of ownership, thus making it more likely the child will work on the goal independently and persist when things feel challenging.

Make Goals Memorable

Some of our clearest memories from childhood are from when we were at play. Why? Because play taps into many of our brain's ways of remembering things: It is visual, it is physical, it is fun, and it is repetitive. If we want our children to invest in goals and carry on independently, use the qualities inherent in play to make the goals memorable. Vygotsky (1978) said, "The very essence of human memory consists in the fact that human beings actively remember with the help of signs" (51). For example, many people put a rubber band around their wrist, or jot themselves a sticky note, or put a reminder into their smartphone to help them remember something important. Children benefit from reminders as well. In her book, *A Quick Guide to Making Your Teaching Stick,* Shanna Schwartz (2008) says that one way we can make our teaching memorable, or "sticky," is to give children "physical representations of learning" (5). We do this all of the time in our classrooms when we create anchor charts to go along with our lessons. We do this so children have a place to refer back to when they are stuck and so that they will be reminded of what was taught. But how do we make sure the charts and tools we introduce actually do the job they are supposed to do and don't just become wallpaper? One way is to make sure that the charts and tools we create are engaging, enticing, and playful.

How Do I Make Playful Tools?

Playful tools are best made by the experts: your children. First, a nonexample. When Kristi was trying to increase the flexibility of some of her readers, she did some quick research on Power Rangers (Figure 8.3), whose influence was reflected on the shirts and in the fantasy play of many of her students. Realizing the Wikipedia page was too convoluted and not interested in watching the show, she read a synopsis of an episode. Seeing a reference to "Zords" and assuming that meant "swords," she printed out a picture of Power Rangers and set out to teach how you could use lots of different strategies, like the Power Rangers use zords and morphers and assorted other paraphernalia. Immediately there was an outcry—the Power Ranger was a JUNGLE FURY POWER RANGER. And the morpher? The MORPHER belonged to the POWER RANGERS SAMURAI. And the zord? Well, it turns out zords are NOTHING like swords, and to suggest that is to invite the scorn of five-year-olds. The takeaway? When it comes to play, know who the experts are: your children.

Get to know your children and really listen to them. We often "hear" what kids are saying, but that doesn't always mean real understanding on our part. We've all seen the spark in kids' eyes and the total connection when they know that you are giving them time to really share their ideas and thoughts with you. That time, combined with thoughtful, probing questions, has enormous value. In *Knowing Literacy* (1997), Peter Johnston argues that active listening helps us to build social imagination—the ability to imagine characters, to predict reactions, and to understand motives. Through this questioning and listening, we come to close the empathy gap and tap into the topics that really motivate children. No matter how cool or playful you think your idea may be, if it is not deeply connected to the world of your children, and not reflective of their own understandings and expertise, it will not help your students grow as people and as thinkers.

Figure 8.3 Power Ranger play in action.

Next we outline a basic process for bringing the mindset of play to more academic work by adapting the tools you create to be more reflective of children's passions. For more about creating tools, we invite you to look further at the books *Smarter Charts* and *Smarter Charts for Math, Science, and Social Studies* (2014) by Kristi Mraz and Marjorie Martinelli.

A Tool by Any Other Name: A Field Guide to Tools

We define a tool as anything that supports a child to work and think with more independence. Before we begin to think about how to make tools more playful, we first need to identify what they might be.

- **Prop:** An item, like a pointer, that triggers a certain action or thought for a child.

- **Chart:** A support made for a whole class to use, usually hangs in the classroom (Figure 8.4).

- **Minichart:** A smaller version of a class-made chart, or an adapted version of a class-made chart for an individual child (Figure 8.5).

- **Splash Card:** Named by math consultant Ryan Dunn, a splash card is a reminder of new learning given to an individual child, often on a sticky note or index card (Figure 8.6).

- **Photo:** Captures a child in a moment of work or play that the child should replicate (i.e., a picture of a child making a tall block tower reminds him he can also work hard to make long books).

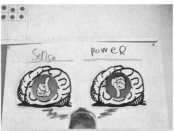

Figure 8.4 A chart made with students.

Figure 8.5 During a conference, this reader is deciding which minichart will make him the most powerful reader he can be.

Figure 8.6 This writer has written the goal he wants to work on for a few weeks on a sticky note.

Ask, "What Tool Can Support This Child with This Skill?"

A tool is never meant to be the most important thing in a lesson, just like the recipe is not the most important thing in a meal. A recipe gets you to the good stuff—the food. A tool gets you to the good stuff—the thinking. Careful planning for how you will introduce and support the actual thinking work will be far more critical than any tool you can develop. However, tools *can* be instrumental in helping children replicate thinking work independently when they need it the most. Some children may need a process to help, and some may need a repertoire of ways to approach a skill. Close listening and careful study are two ways to determine which might work best for the whole class or an individual child.

When introducing a process, we recommend that you do all the teaching in one day, and that any chart or tool have all the steps needed (Figure 8.7). Imagine teaching someone to brush her teeth—you would never give her just the first step. "OK, get your toothbrush wet . . . all right, that's it for today!" The same is true for teaching a process like figuring out an unknown word or using an open number line. A tool or chart that supports a process is designed to help a child achieve a complex task, and will often have numbers and visuals showing each step.

On the other hand, a repertoire tool or chart is all about showing options that help students develop flexibility. Learners are empowered when they have multiple strategies to attack the same challenge. For a real-world example, consider driving to your workplace. If one road is shut down, you likely have other options for how to get there. A roadblock cannot literally or figuratively stop you from reaching your goal, and the same is true for any skill with a repertoire of strategies. When you introduce these tools and charts, you'll be teaching several strategies or techniques at once.

When considering which tool makes the most sense for your class or for an individual child, consider whether flexibility is needed to achieve a skill, or whether a complicated process needs to

Figure 8.7 A process chart for a math strategy.

Figure 8.8 A repertoire chart for nonfiction text features.

be broken down into smaller steps. Determining which is right will mean a more sticky and meaningful support.

Some children may just need an engaging prop or picture to trigger their recall of the repertoire or process they need to access; others may need more detailed, supportive charts (Figure 8.8), but all children need to be part of the process of developing their tool.

Investigate: "How Can I Connect This to the Interests and Play Themes I See in My Classroom?"

We see children get into character all the time. They step into high heels and start using the word *Dahling*, or they put on a police badge and race around making siren noises. Small items can trigger play, and as teachers, we can use this knowledge to make all work more playful and to leverage powerful thinking. Authentic and active listening to your students will ensure any charts and tools are grounded in their true interests and are not just "cool" because we think they are cool. For a child who loves Pokemon, a lightsaber pointer (no matter how cool it is) won't necessarily lead to deeper and more reflective work. The most meaningful supports are the ones children actively participate in creating.

Can the Tool Look Like Something Children Know from Play?

In a world of Ninjago, Teenage Mutant Ninja Turtles, Power Rangers, and many more, swords and weapons hold sway over many children. Rather than eliminate them from the classroom and deny children a right to their interests, reimagine them into tools for learning (Figure 8.9). For the Star Wars loving child, pipe cleaners as lightsabers provide a powerful incentive to chop up tricky words in reading. Similarly, children who love to play doctor may find a lab coat a powerful motivator to give their writing a "check-up." Wristbands with paper buttons and pens taped to look like lightsabers may feel silly, but they are powerful in the hands of the right child. When the tools children need are connected to the play themes they love, the tools immediately become more powerful and motivating for children to use.

Other Possible Tools:

- "Baseball" cards with strategies
- Minecraft tools repurposed for support with reading or writing
- Paper smartphones with strategies as "apps"

Can You Use an Analogy to Something Children Do or Love in Play?

In Alison's kindergarten classroom, it became the work of many, many days to make a spaceship that consisted of every single Unifix cube attached end to end. The center drew maps of where it could go, split into teams, tried to make it reach from table to table, until they settled on keeping it on the floor. After days of labor, the spaceship reached unbroken from the rug to outside the classroom door, and the entire classroom erupted in cheers. Alison snapped a picture and placed it on the easel to tell the story of the epic spaceship. Later that same day, she brought it back up at writing time by asking, "How is writing like making this spaceship?" The children were bursting with ideas, from the literal— "You can keep getting more paper to make your story longer"—to the more abstract—"You can change your story to be different like we made the spaceship different." Pictures from children's play remind them that they can use the same mindsets whether they are working with blocks or books, dress-up costumes or writing paper, cardboard boxes or math problems.

Figure 8.9 A bandana prop (inspired by Teenage Mutant Ninja Turtles) supports a reader's expertise at chopping words.

Analogies can also be drawn to the more imaginary worlds children create. When reading gets tricky, equating a reader's many strategies to Iron Man's flexibility with weapons can engage a child in more vigorous and intentional strategy work. Analogies can drive points home in powerful ways and give abstract ideas a concrete counterpoint in the world of play.

Other Possible Analogies:

- Batman and Robin as models for how partners work together.
- The transition of Padawan to Jedi to reinforce the role of practice.
- A doctor's check-up as an analogy for editing writing.

Can a Meaningful Visual Be Incorporated from Something Children Know and Love?

In conversation with a kindergartener one morning, Katie learned something interesting about the character Rainbow Dash from My Little Pony: According to Gabriela, she was very optimistic. Asked for examples, Gabriela explained how in the episode she just watched, Rainbow Dash was brave enough to try something before all the other ponies did. Katie tucked this information away until it was time to help Gabriela in writing, where she often sat frozen. Katie used the picture of Rainbow Dash on Gabriela's tool for getting writing ideas as a reminder that she, too, could be optimistic. Sticking a picture of a My Little Pony on a tool may invite an interested child to use it, but choosing a picture that is meaningful in its intent will make it even more powerful. Children treasure high-interest visuals, so consider using clip art, Google images, and children's own drawings to decorate their tools and increase their engagement with them (Figure 8.10).

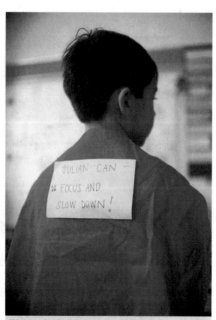

Figure 8.10 This reader designed a cape to help him remember to be Super Reader.

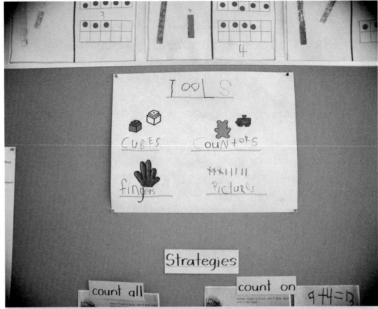

Figure 8.11 A student-designed math tools chart.

Can a Child Design the Tool or Chart?

Simply asking, "What might we need to help us do _____?" can start a conversation about tools and charts that is completely led by children. As adults, we may assume we know what will best help a child, but that is not always the case. Inviting children to design a tool or a chart (Figure 8.11) teaches them a much larger lesson: We all need things to help us from time to time, and you can make those things yourself. Having children make their own tools, with support and guidance as needed, sends a message about agency and power—namely that children possess it.

Peek into the Classroom:
Playful Tools Promote Big Thinking

It feels like the first blast of autumn on this cloudy and windy October morning in first grade. Up to 40 percent of the class has special needs, so a general-education teacher and a special educator coteach all twenty-eight students all day. Children are positioned cozily around the room, some in bean bags, some at tables, some even curled up in the alcove beneath the sink, reading books and murmuring occasionally to their partners nearby. Kathryn, one of the two teachers in this integrated classroom, has quietly gathered a group of four boys to the small rainbow rug in the back of the room. She knows all four of these children tend to freeze up or mumble over tricky words in their books. She also knows that these four boys can often be found huddled over Legos reenacting the *Clone Wars* from Star Wars at choice time, passionately arguing the relative strength of various characters.

Notice How . . .

* Classroom space is used to mimic how reading occurs in the real world—casually and comfortably.
* Reading groups are pulled flexibly and with a common goal.
* The teacher knows her children on multiple levels—both as readers and as players—and this knowledge helps her organize grouping.

Kathryn begins her conversation with these boys first in the arena of play, quickly engaging them by asking, "What do you think makes a good Jedi?" The boys leap to answer with ideas varying from types of lightsaber to years of fighting experience before quickly settling into a general adoration of Darth Maul's double lightsaber, despite the fact he is not a Jedi but a member of the Dark Side. Kathryn begins to transition the conversation to reading by asking, "So, what do Jedis do when they come to big problems?"

Notice How . . .

* The teacher is engaging the students' interests in play so their energy is positive and excited.
* The teacher is asking questions and letting the children be the experts (which they are!).

The boys mention that Jedis can work together, they use the force, they fight when they need to, and sometimes, when the opponent is really strong, they may even lose at first, but then they keep fighting. Kathryn's face lights up, as though she is having an idea for the first time. "Oh my gosh," she says. "You know, as you are talking, I am realizing YOU are like READING JEDIS! You guys can work together, you can figure out tricky words, and when something in a book is hard, you don't give up! Right?" The boys nod. "Wait, though," Kathryn continues. "You need something if you are going to be a reading Jedi." She rummages behind her back and reveals with great flourish little lightsabers made of pipe cleaners. "Lightsabers!"

The boys gasp with delight and grab them. Kathryn has made them in a variety of colors—red, green, blue, and purple—and the boys root through them to find the color of their favorite character.

Kathryn begins again, "So we know how Jedis use real-size lightsabers, but how would reading Jedis use reading lightsabers, I wonder?"

Notice How . . .

* The tool replicates something the children know and love from play.
* There is choice within the tool (the color).
* The teacher does not at first dictate the way the tool must be used. She allows for exploration and inquiry into its potential.

"We could use it to point at the words!" one of the boys says and demonstrates on his book.

"Or the picture!" says another.

"Or to cover up the words!"

This is the opening Kathryn was waiting for, and she uses it to segue into the strategy she thinks will help the boys gain confidence in the harder books they have now started reading.

Notice How . . .

* The children rename strategies they have already learned (e.g., point to the words, pictures), but the tool has re-engaged them.
* The teacher looks for an organic opening into introducing a strategy—if the segue had not occurred naturally, she would have introduced it more directly.

Kathryn stops the boys and says, "Hmmm, cover up the word, or even, cover up *part* of the word? Sometimes when words are realllllllly long, they can feel scary to try to read, but we can use our lightsabers to chop up a word and then we can try to figure out the first part by thinking about what would make sense in the story." Kathryn quickly demonstrates in a book with the word *spaghetti*. The sentence reads: *I eat spaghetti for breakfast*.

Kathryn covers up the ***hetti*** with her lightsaber leaving only ***spag*** visible and reads the sentence, thinking aloud, "What could make sense?" The reading Jedis know immediately and begin shouting "Spaghetti! Spaghetti! Spaghetti!"

Kathryn smiles and says, "Prove it, reading Jedis! How do you know for sure?"

Notice How . . .

* The teacher is teaching a fairly straightforward strategy for readers in F books, but the tool and the language have made it more playful.
* The tool is used in a meaningful way that will help the readers tackle longer words.

continues

continued

Figure 8.12 Choosing and using a tool for reading partners.

Kathryn asks the Jedi readers to try it in their own books and coaches as each of the boys tries it. As with all tools, the reading lightsaber is getting used way more than it is needed, but Kathryn sees a new determination in these readers to try to make sense of the longer, more intimidating words in their books. She sends the boys off with the suggestion that they teach their partners how reading Jedis conquer words, and with the hint that they may even become reading Yodas.

Figure 8.13 Making swords to use as pointers later.

Plato wisely once said, "Do not keep children to their studies by compulsion but by play." Why is there a line drawn between play and work? Is the reading work done by Kathryn's first graders any less meaningful than work done without a sense of lightness and joy? No, it's not. The goal of creating lifelong readers is the same in many first-grade classrooms, but when we choose meaningful, playful tools to help us reach that goal, we honor that we are teaching children. And as teachers, it is our job to teach the living, breathing, delightfully unique children in front of us. It is not our job to bend our children to curriculum but to bend the curriculum to our children. Infusing a sense of play into the teeniest corners of the day, from singing a silly song to transition to reimagining pointers as lightsabers, means that we celebrate children while still meeting standards.

INQUIRY IS A PLAY MINDSET
Learning How to Learn

I think, at a child's birth, if a mother could ask a fairy godmother to endow it with the most useful gift, that gift should be curiosity.
—Eleanor Roosevelt

As Cheryl surveyed the classroom during choice time, she observed first graders engaged in all kinds of discoveries. Some kids were busy figuring out how to stimulate snails to race. (Research suggested beer!) Others were mixing paint for signs for the bookstore study. Still others were building shelves out of blocks to replicate the bookstore. Admittedly, she basked in a bit of pride to see how well they were collaborating, negotiating, and independently problem solving.

In these times of play, there were "aha" moments as children sorted out the answers to questions they had, and yet, this energy seemed to be missing during the rest of the day. The academic work children were doing was important, but it also felt literal and seemed to lack depth. Cheryl loved the idea of teaching kids the process of inquiry but had always been a bit reluctant, envisioning chaos with kids off exploring their unique passions. Truth be told, she wasn't certain that it was manageable with twenty-eight five- and six-year-olds and one teacher.

But who doesn't love those "aha" moments? Cheryl felt her own when she signed up for professional development offered through the Museum of Natural History located a few blocks from her school. The museum was featuring an exhibit on tiles, and teachers were going to learn how to share the learning with the kids in their classrooms. They learned about tiles, and then the instructor told the group that they were each going to take an aspect of the exhibit and answer several questions; Cheryl's was on how tiles were manufactured. Cheryl dutifully took her clipboard with the questions and went off to complete the assignment.

She answered the questions in five or six minutes and then stood there with that "I'm done" look on her face. The problem was that she wasn't much interested in her assigned topic. What really intrigued her was the part of the exhibit with photos and models of how tiles were used to decorate castles in nineteenth-century France. She wandered over to that section of the exhibit and spent the next fifty minutes focused on noticing, wondering, asking questions, and developing ideas about those castles that fascinated her. And while Cheryl was doing that, she began to realize that the process of inquiry is a perspective on learning that begins with an intense curiosity, a curiosity that generates close observation, noticings, wonderings, and questions that lead to new and interesting ideas.

Play invites inquiry, and inquiry accepts that invitation. In play kids have the opportunities to linger, to examine, to wonder, to notice, to look closely, to ask why things are the way they are, and to share their thinking. By giving children space and time to play you will see what they know, what they can do, and what they want to learn about. Children playing with blocks ask questions that lead to explorations of simple machines, force and motion, and engineering. Children naturally build the world around them, and in re-creating the bookstore, the dollar store, and the local restaurant, their actions fuel questions about communities, needs and wants, and change over time. Through play, children explore and express their ideas, interests, and passions with inquiry as a natural and authentic partner in the process. Play brings inquiry, but does inquiry as an instructional method bring play?

In short, yes. Inquiry injects a play mindset into all learning because it is a process that occurs when playing. Setting off to answer big questions through observation and experimentation is a more formal description of an inherently natural process. Who among us did not approximate this idea as we set up our bathroom cabinets as laboratories, wondering, what if I add mouthwash to baby powder? And for the more daring—I wonder what this neon concoction tastes like? So how do we transition this playful, natural approach to learning from its natural habitat to the parameters of school? How do we make all learning feel like play? The answer is: through an inquiry approach (Figure 9.1).

Inquiry: An Exploration

If you want to understand inquiry as a process, all you have to do is watch a toddler puzzle over some new discovery. One morning Alison's sixteen-month-old son Preston was playing with a mirror when he noticed a light reflecting and bouncing on the ceiling. He stared inquisitively, seeming to wonder where the light came from. Preston looked closely at the things around him and then noticed that when he moved the mirror, the reflection on the ceiling moved too. He picked up the mirror and turned it so it faced the wall, as if to ask, "I wonder if it will do the same thing if I move the mirror this way?" With a furrowed brow, he moved the mirror again and again, this way and that, until his theory was confirmed. A satisfied look crossed his face, and he was ready to move on and discover the next thing.

Figure 9.1 Playing and experimenting with blocks leads to questions about simple machines.

Just as a toddler playfully explores his world for the first time, scientists and social scientists follow a similar process to develop new understandings about our world. According to the National Science Teachers Association (2004), "inquiry reflects how scientists come to understand the natural world, and it is at the heart of how students learn. From a very early age, children interact with their environment, ask questions, and seek ways to answer those questions. Understanding science content is significantly enhanced when ideas are anchored to inquiry experiences." As Preston so aptly demonstrated, children are born with a natural tendency for inquiry, and there is no boundary between their play and the thoughtful experimentation that leads to new understandings. They are one and the same. Now, you may think that the rigorous experimentation that happens in a science lab is quite different from children's natural inquiry, but in fact it retains two key features: It begins in curiosity and then moves forward with a spirit of playfulness, a willingness to see "what happens if . . ." The stories of two Nobel Prize winners bear this out.

When Alexander Fleming noticed some curious mold growing on a flu culture, he examined the sample more closely and observed that the mold actually killed the bacteria it was touching in the dish (Krock 2001). He ran some more tests to confirm his theory and ended up receiving the Nobel Prize for discovering the antibiotic, penicillin—a world-changing discovery that began with a simple curiosity.

Physicist Richard Feynman said his theory about the interaction between light and matter was discovered through play. "It was effortless. It was easy to play with these things. It was like uncorking a bottle: Everything flowed out effortlessly. I almost tried to resist it! There was no importance to what I was doing, but ultimately there was. The diagrams and the whole business that I got the Nobel Prize for came from that piddling around with the wobbling plate" (1997, 67). The development of quantum electrodynamics came from "piddling around."

In the classroom, inquiry is an approach to instruction that mimics the process by which humans naturally learn. As a methodology, inquiry begins in curiosity, moves forward with a spirit of playful experimentation, and is nothing like the top-down textbook-driven approach so many of us experienced during our schooling. The National Council for Social Studies developed a framework for Social Studies State Standards in 2013. A major part of the framework states that rich social studies teaching allows students to develop and investigate their own questions through "disciplinary and multidisciplinary means" (17). Similarly the National Science Teachers Association (2004) recommends that all teachers "embrace scientific inquiry and is committed to helping educators make it the centerpiece of the science classroom."

How the Principles and Processes of Play and Inquiry Intertwine

Working together, inquiry and play create a joyful partnership. That partnership is fundamental when we reflect on our beliefs about the children we teach and how they learn. We have come to understand that kids learn best

- when they have choice.
- when they collaborate.
- when they have ownership over learning.
- when experiences are open-ended.
- when they know it is OK to take risks.
- when they don't just answer the questions of others but develop their own wonderings and questions.

Figure 9.2 Amazement over making a car ramp leads to a conversation around force and motion.

- when they experiment with newly developing ideas.
- when they share insights and learning with friends.
- when they replicate their learning and construct meaning with words, stories, drama, building, drawing, painting, sculpture, music, and play.
- when learning connects to their passions, hearts, and imagination.

Essentially, these beliefs grow from trust. We trust that kids are strong and capable. We trust that they construct meaning by negotiating with their environment through play. And we trust their curiosity will lead them to discovery and ideas that seem to unfold magically as they did when a group of third-grade children came to wonder how they could make cars go farther on the ramps they had built with blocks (Figure 9.2).

The Inquiry Process

Begin with Curiosity

Judith Wells Lindfors (1999) states, "Acts of inquiry stand as the ultimate act of going beyond: going beyond present understanding (intellectual); going beyond self to engage the help of another (social) but even going beyond as self (personal) (14)." In the classroom, the inquiry process (Figure 9.3) follows a predictable set of steps; however, most educators agree that the process is recursive in nature, rather than linear.

The process always begins with students' curiosity about something. Now, right away you might be wondering, "How is that possible or realistic in this day of standards? How can a teacher wait to see what students are curious about and still have time to teach what is required in the curriculum?" The answer lies somewhere in between. A teacher's role in a standards-based inquiry classroom is to plant seeds of curiosity for her students based on what is required in the curriculum. For example, in New York City, second graders are required to learn about plant diversity as part of the second-grade science curriculum. Rather than saying to her students, "Class, this month we are learning about plants. Let me teach you about the parts first," which is how many of us learned. Michelle Hernandez, a teacher in the South Bronx, took a more playful, inquiry approach to the study. She kicked off the study by placing some plants on the classroom inquiry table for students to observe when they came in first thing in the morning and during times of play. She left blank sheets of paper and ebony pencils so students could sketch and write down their thoughts, wonderings, and observations.

Students observed and jotted down their noticings for a few days, and then Michelle began to notice a pattern in their discussions and jottings. Many students began wondering why some plants had flowers and some did not. Michelle saw that their curiosity had been sparked, so the next day she brought in flowering and nonflowering plants for each table in the classroom so they could dig in a little

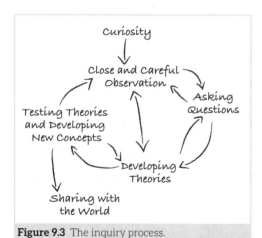

Figure 9.3 The inquiry process.

deeper with their study. Michelle set up her students to engage with the topic in a firsthand way, which piqued their interest and set them on a path toward a rich inquiry study.

When beginning a study in any area, it helps to start with a photo, text, video, or object that brings out curiosity and intrigue. A collection of images or objects spread across tables with the simple instruction to observe and wonder can begin to generate much of the heat that will drive the rest of the study. At times our instructions may be more specific—"What do you notice and wonder about the parts of these plants?"—or more open-ended—"What do you notice and wonder about these images?" Inviting discovery creates the conditions of a play mindset as children launch themselves into the work of investigation.

Close and Careful Observation

The next step of the process involves teaching students how to do some close and careful observations so that they can develop more focused questions (Figure 9.4). In her class, Michelle gave each of her students a magnifying glass and taught them some strategies for how to observe closely. She taught strategies such as zooming in and looking part by part and using your senses to think about color, shape, size, and texture. Students sketched and recorded their observations, which they housed in their inquiry folders. As Michelle conferred, she kept a copy of the science standards for the unit on her clipboard so she was sure to ask questions to angle students' observations, if necessary. For example, she prompted students not just to look at the parts of one plant but to compare the different parts across plants.

Once students do some close observations they are ready to develop some informed questions that can lead to focused investigations and research. If real objects are hard to come by, children can observe photographs instead (Figure 9.5).

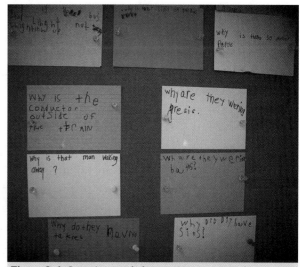

Figure 9. 4 Questions and observations are posted to revisit later in the study.

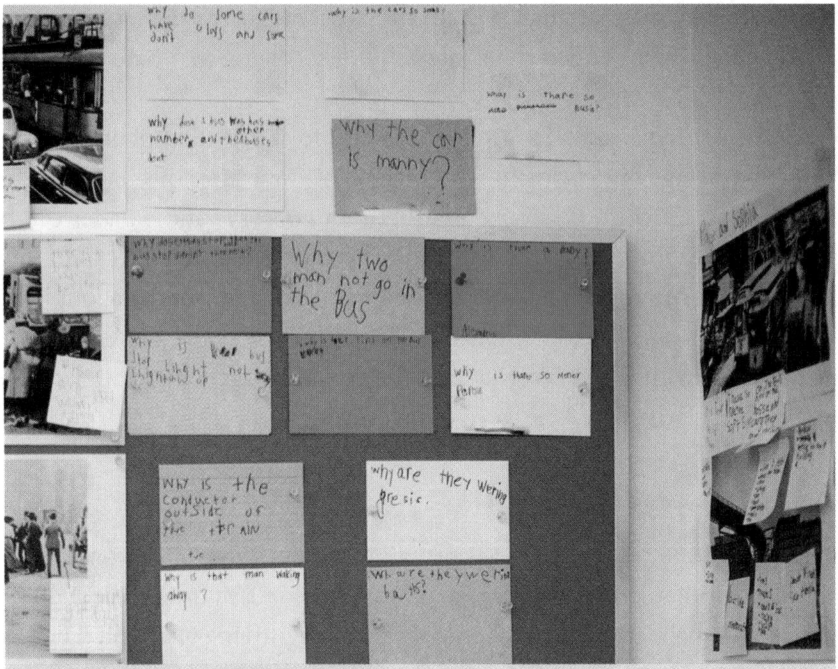

Figure 9.5 A close study of photographs prompted wonderings about New York City's past.

Ask Questions

In Michelle's class, students' close observations of plants led them to wonder about things such as, "Why are there white dots on the leaves?" and "Why is the plant growing on the right side of the container?" It's important to teach students about the role of questions in an inquiry. Any question that students wonder about is a good question and worthy of investigation. You can teach kids that powerful questions should be open to research, might have several answers, and may lead to more questions. Also, be sure to name what students are doing with their questions. "You asked why there are white dots on the leaves. That's the kind of question that might lead to more questions."

Nekia Wise, upper-grade science teacher at PS 59 in Manhattan, talks about the importance of understanding how to investigate questions that come from inquiry. As students ask questions, Nekia records them all on a chart, and then she and the students go back through together to categorize them. Which questions can be answered in a snap, which questions are really big questions that would be hard to find the answer to (e.g., what came first, the chicken or the egg?), and which questions might be answered if we did more research and even conducted experiments? After categorizing the questions, the class picks a few "investigatable" questions to study. At this point in the process, it helps to consult the standards to see which questions will lead you toward the key ideas in the curriculum. For example, Michelle's class chose to investigate why some of the plants were growing toward one side of the container and others were not, a question that would address the standard about how plants respond to changes in their environment.

Once noticings and questions have been gathered, teachers have a choice to pursue questions as a whole class (easier for those newer to inquiry) or in small groups, depending on children's interests. Materials you may have used to teach directly in the past (videos, expert visits, field trips, books, images) can now be used to help children find answers to the questions they have generated. It feels magical to uncover an answer to something you have been wondering. Utilize whole-class lessons and small-group instruction to refine students' thinking and build the skills required in inquiry. If the thinking seems surface level, like when children's questions can be answered with a simple yes or no, or when children quickly feel "done," you might pull small groups to encourage deeper thinking. When meeting with children, consider asking questions such as

- What did you notice about what you were observing?
- Why do you think it's like that?
- Where did you get that idea?
- What makes you think so?
- What questions and wonderings do you have about that?
- How and where can you gather more information to confirm or revise your ideas?
- What new discoveries do you plan to learn more about?

Small groups will engage in collaborative conversations to share their wonderings and ideas, and these conversations are an essential part of the inquiry process. There may be times when it is not just thinking you are teaching into but a myriad of skills and concepts.

Developing Theories

With focused questions in hand, students are ready to develop some theories. A theory can be as simple as an idea and a reason for having that idea: "Maybe some plants grow toward the side because there's more sun there." In Michelle Hernandez's class children generated multiple theories about plants in a number of ways. First they took their questions and did more close observation, jotting down their theories in their inquiry folders. Next the class engaged in an academic conversation where students shared, built upon, challenged, and defended one another's theories. This kind of conversation often leads to new theories being developed, as well as new questions for students to pursue.

In their book *Inquiry at the Window* (1997), Phyllis and David Whitin emphasize that it's important for kids to understand that "exploring theories is rough draft thinking and that they [are] allowed to revise their thinking at any point along the way" (51). Framing a theory with "it might be" or "maybe" helps children understand that these ideas are open to ongoing change. When learners develop multiple theories it allows them to be flexible thinkers, and it often leads to more questions and more theories. "Multiple theories have the potential to widen the vision of how learners interpret the world" (53).

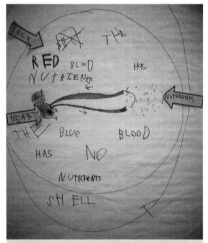

Figure 9.6 A group of kindergarteners, curious about the veins they could see when candling their chicken eggs, set out on an inquiry to discover what the veins did. This is the diagram they made to teach their classmates.

Testing Theories and Discovering New Concepts

When students have developed some theories, they are ready to do some investigating to confirm or revise them. In Michelle's classroom, students investigated in a number of ways. They pored through books on the topic, they conducted experiments, and they returned to the local florist shop where they could consult with experts. Researching with books and videos, talking in academic conversations, conducting interviews, examining photos closely, and sketching are all ways children can gather more information about their theories (Figure 9.6).

As students confirmed and revised their theories, they often found themselves having new questions and new theories to test. For example, in Michelle's class the students wondered if all plants would grow toward light or just the particular kind they had planted? They went on to test this theory with a few varieties of plants and discovered that only certain plants grew toward the light.

The process of inquiry was exhilarating for students, and to them it felt as natural as all the playing and discovering they had been doing their whole lives before coming to school.

Sharing with the World

Most inquiry studies culminate with presenting the findings to others, and the possibilities for this are many. Students might create a poster or an oral presentation, write a nonfiction book about the topic, create a teaching video, or recreate the learning in blocks, drama, or art. In Michelle's class, students created posters to summarize their learning and then invited their upper-grade buddies to the classroom so they could orally present their findings. The documentation students construct to present their findings helps you assess the depth of their understanding. The big idea is for children to synthesize their learning and live the life of scientists or social scientists by being an active part of a collaborative learning and teaching community.

Decide on Topics for In-Depth Inquiry

One of the beautiful things about young children is that they are naturally inquisitive. They are curious about why the elevator keeps breaking down in school and what the safety agent's walkie-talkie is used for. They wonder why the class pet hamster twitches his nose and what is happening with the construction down the street. It can be hard to sift through all these curiosities to find the thing that will sustain an in-depth inquiry study. By reflecting on our own more and less successful experiences with inquiry in the classroom, we've learned a few things that now help guide our decision making.

Provide a Platform for Wondering

In their book *A Place for Wonder* (2009), Georgia Heard and Jennifer McDonough talk about creating a space in the classroom for students to jot down their wonderings.

It can be something as simple as a piece of chart paper with some sticky notes and pens nearby, or it could be a section of an inquiry notebook or folder. Whatever the structure, the important thing is giving students space to write down their big questions. Having this kind of space in the classroom sends the implicit message that this classroom values students' questions and expects students to have questions. This space will give you a window into your students' curiosities, and you will be able to easily see which questions come up over and over again. Once you have a sense for your students' burning questions, you can use them to kick off an inquiry study. For example, some teachers start a class meeting by sharing a particular wondering that has come up a lot and then invite students to come up with theories and ways they can discover the answer to their wonderings. Other teachers use the wonderings as a genesis for stocking the inquiry table, or filling up a book display case with books on the topic, or planning a field trip.

Connect to Students' Interests

As mentioned throughout this book, students' interests are at the heart of making the classroom a more joyful place for students to learn. Inquiry always starts with learners' interest and curiosity in something. While teachers often place materials in the classroom to generate curiosity (as Michelle did with plants), just as often, children *bring* curiosity in with them. For example, playing "pet store" became a popular play theme in Danielle's first-grade class when the families of Janel, Cahle, and Shakira brought new pets into their homes.

While building shelves out of hollow blocks and making signs "Kittens and Puppies for Sale," Antoine offered, "My grandma says that it's better to get pets at the shelter because they need a home."

Denise chimed in, "That's where I got Bailey—at the ASPCA. He was living on the street, and somebody found him and took him there so we gave him a home."

Anna looked perplexed and said, "Well, we bought Billy (her kitten) at the pet store on 149th Street."

At share meeting that day the pet store/shelter theme launched a lively conversation, and there was a barrage of stories about where family pets came from. Since learning about the neighborhood was part of the first-grade social studies curriculum, Danielle seized upon the excitement this topic generated to launch an inquiry study of a local rescue organization and the neighborhood pet store (which many children passed each day on their way to school). There were dozens of wonderings including: "How do animals get in the shelter? What's the difference between a shelter and a pet store? What happens to animals that don't get adopted?" Playing "pet store" during choice time sparked a whole-class inquiry study based on kids' keen interests.

Plant Seeds and See Which Roots Take Hold

We all have standards and core curriculum to address. However, most content area units of study are broad enough to leave lots of room to tailor instruction to children's interests. As we saw in the example from Michelle Hernandez's second-grade classroom, before a unit of study begins the teacher can spark students' interest in a topic by giving a preview. Michelle's classroom had an inquiry table, and across the year Michelle would place various objects or photographs and invite the children to observe, notice, and wonder about them. At some times in the year the items would connect to a required content area study, and at other times Michelle would invite students to stock the inquiry table based on their interests from home. The only requirement was that the items relate to science or social studies. Her students brought in everything from pinecones and seashells to maps and travel brochures. As students observe, jot, and discuss their noticings from the inquiry table, you can listen for patterns in students' questions and thoughts to get a sense for which curiosities might take hold. When a question or a concept comes up again and again, you have found your inquiry study.

Building New Skills Through Inquiry

There are often two strands of lessons in an inquiry study: process and content. Process lessons are designed to teach step-by-step skills that will enable children to access deeper thinking. As these processes become habit, children will begin to use them naturally across the day (see Figure 9.7). Content lessons help students understand ideas or information relevant to the topic, and they are often taught through direct instruction because they aid the larger inquiry work.

Teaching points for process might include

- How to observe and look closely.
- How looking closely takes time (the importance of lingering).

- How to share noticings with friends.

- How to develop theories and ideas about our noticings.

- How to use additional information to confirm or revise our theories.

- How to replicate what we have learned to share with others.

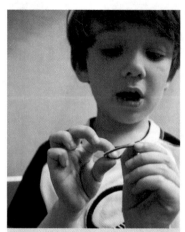

Figure 9.7 Looking closely and wondering about an object in the recess yard.

It's important to include lessons about the content of the study as well. You don't want misinformation to stand. If kids are not clear about an idea or have a misconception, you will want to bring it back to the inquiry process to ensure that kids are revising ideas that don't stand up to evidence. For example, if children have a theory that dads work and moms stay home, it is our responsibility to provide materials and experiences that help them challenge and revise that hypothesis.

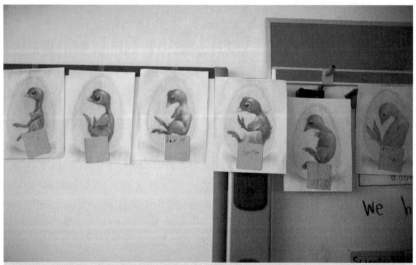

Figure 9.8 An inquiry about chicken embryo development irons out confusion in children's thinking that chicks look the same but just get bigger in the egg.

How Do I Make All Kinds of Learning More Discovery-Based?

In "Exploring Inquiry as a Teaching Stance in the Writing Workshop" (2006), Katie Wood Ray explains, "Framing instruction in this way represents an essential stance to teaching and learning, an inquiry stance, characterized by repositioning curriculum as the outcome of instruction rather than as the starting point" (239). These powerful words require a moment of reflection. How often have we started with goals and specified outcomes only to question why kids weren't "getting it"? How often have we felt the frustration that our carefully crafted lessons weren't sticking? Almost anything can be repositioned as inquiry if we start first with children's observations and questions and end with understandings (Figure 9.8). We borrow the methods of inquiry teaching and bring them into our focus lessons and conferences and small groups during all parts of our day. By doing so we can build upon our learners' playful, inquisitive stances to help them discover and solidify learning in all subject areas (Figure 9.9). Never underestimate the engagement potential of the questions, "What do you see? What do you wonder? What do you think?" It may be investigating patterns in words during word study, trying to understand the difference between dollars and cents, or noticing how an author uses punctuation during shared reading. By taking an inquiry stance during the day we are enabling explorations that are authentic, abundant, and, most important, have meaning for each learner.

Teaching through inquiry is essentially the opposite of direct instruction, and which method you use depends on your purpose. Even when engaged in an inquiry study, direct instruction may still be needed at times, such as when teaching explicit strategies for how to observe and question.

Figure 9.9 A money inquiry develops as children learn about the stores in their local community.

Direct Instruction Method vs. Inquiry Method

Method of Instruction	Direct Instruction	Inquiry
Feature	Name what you are going to teach, and then explain and/or demonstrate how.	Show an example, and ask students what they notice.
Example	Readers, today I am going to teach you how to use the picture to figure out the meaning of this unknown word. Watch how I do this . . .	Readers, we are going to watch this video of Caitlin figuring out an unknown word. As you watch try to think about what strategies you see her using.

Peek into the Classroom:
Inquiry into the Neighborhood

When Nekia was a first-grade teacher, she took her class on a trip to the 99 Cent Store. They were engaged in an in-depth study about the neighborhood, and it was the third time they had visited the store. Nekia had carefully planned the neighborhood unit and felt that while kids seemed engaged, they needed deeper understanding and more ownership over their learning.

The 99 Cent Store was a place most of the kids knew well because their families shopped there, and Nekia had also seen children building it at choice time. Since the store was right around the corner from the school, it also met the criteria of being a place they could visit frequently to gather more information to revise and confirm their theories. And so the 99 Cent Store became the focus of their inquiry study.

Usually, trips began with a class discussion where kids answered two questions posed by Nekia: "What do you know about the place we are visiting?" and "What do you want to know about the place we are visiting?" This time, instead of starting with these predetermined questions, Nekia wanted kids to begin the inquiry with their own observations. The important work they had to do at the 99 Cent Store was to notice, observe, and look closely at everything that piqued their curiosity.

Notice How . . .

* The teacher used a location that met the criteria for social studies curriculum as a vehicle to engage in the inquiry process.
* The teacher opened up possibilities for exploration by asking children to notice closely, thus closely linking the study to children's interests.

Upon returning from their first trip to the 99 Cent Store, Nekia charted all the students' wonderings and questions. The wonderings included:

* Where do the workers sleep at night when the store closes? Do they stay in the store?
* What is the big camera on the ceiling for?
* Why is it called a 99 Cent Store when lots of stuff costs more than ninety-nine cents?

At this point in the study each child in the classroom joined a group based on his or her own wonderings. The groups met with Nekia for small-group collaborative conversations to talk about the theories they had developed about these questions.

The group exploring where the workers sleep at night developed a theory that they slept on beds in the back of the store to make sure the store was safe. Before their next trip Nekia met with them, and they discussed tools and strategies they could use to revise or confirm their theory. They created questions to interview the workers, and they decided to ask to see in the back of the store so they could confirm or revise their theory.

continues

continued

Notice How . . .

* The teacher validated childrens' ideas and didn't correct a misconception but coached them in using tools to gather more information.

When they returned from their next visit, Nekia started the conversation with, "So, what did you guys learn today? Does what you learned mean that you can confirm your theory, or does it need to be revised?" Samuel and Jamale started by reading the responses to the interview questions they had designed. Nekia then prompted them, "So, does that information mean that you need to revise your original theory?" The group agreed they needed to revise their theory. Tameeka and Will shared that they went to the back of the store, and there were no beds, but there was a place where the workers ate. They also shared that there was lots of "stuff" in the back of the store. The group wanted to know what was there and why it was there and agreed that would be their next exploration.

Notice How . . .

* The process of inquiry is circular: Answers often lead to more questions.
* The teacher coached into revision.
* Children share their learning so all gain the understanding, even though they pursued personal questions.

The final stage and ongoing work of the inquiry study was building the 99 Cent Store in their classroom during choice time. Shelves were built from blocks, kids took on different jobs, signs were made, and items for sale came from home and were priced. Playing "store" evolved from a general script to replicating the specific neighborhood store based on their observations, noticings, and research. The 99 Cent Store included the back room where workers could eat and merchandise was stored. Children priced the items to reflect a range greater than 99 cents and debated if it was fair to call it the 99 Cent Store. Workers used the language of retail that they learned from the employees, and play extended from just selling to ordering merchandise and paying bills. Replication is a powerful assessment to determine how kids have used play and the inquiry process to share their learning.

Meanwhile, Nekia noticed that another inquiry could begin after children's indignation on the first trip to the 99 Cent Store. Every child had a dollar to spend, and that dollar didn't cover the cost of some of the items they had selected. This mismatch between what was said and what was possible opened the door to an inquiry around advertising.

Notice How . . .

* One inquiry often leads to another inquiry.
* Simple questions such as "Where do the workers sleep?" can lead to complex understandings, in this case supply and demand.
* Play illustrates children's understandings.

Inquiry is a process that begins with an intense curiosity. The power of inquiry is that, like play, it often takes us to a place that was never imagined. Listen to kids, and follow their questions and wonderings. Nekia followed kids' lead when a 99 Cent Store study sparked the realization that advertising can be misleading.

High-stakes testing—it rules much of today's educational policy. Test prep that teaches kids to bubble in the correct answer has become an integral part of curriculum. But don't we want far more for our kids? It's not nearly enough for children to simply answer the questions of others. We want them to be the ones asking the questions and challenging and pushing back when the answers don't make sense. Inquiry, because it is inherently playful and involves the same principles as play, fosters a perspective on learning that thrives on curiosity, builds on children's strengths, and gives voice to all learners.

Closing Thoughts

Our mindset is everything. It shapes how we see the world, make decisions, and confront challenge. Our mindset is also ours to mold. When we wake up each morning, we have choices: to choose joy or to choose pessimism, to choose engagement or to choose complacency, to choose hope or to choose fear. But we never need to choose between play and work. In our classrooms, and in the world, we can bring the optimism, enthusiasm, and improvisation of play to all aspects of our work with children and adults. Childhood happens but once, and we can be its protectors, its advocates, and its champions (Figure 9.10). Choose joy, choose engagement, choose hope, choose inquiry, choose play. Every child. Every day.

Figure 9.10 The sheer joy of play is an essential part of childhood.

APPENDIX A

STAGES OF FANTASY PLAY

Debra Leong and Elena Bodrova are a wonderful resource for the stages of play. In their article in *Young Children* (2012), "Assessing and Scaffolding Make Believe Play," they categorized five stages of play, specific to make-believe play.

1. **First Scripts.** In this stage, the pretend play is focused on an object, such as picking up a pretend phone and saying, "Hello?"

2. **Roles in Action.** The child's pretend role is a result of playing with an object or material. For example, a child stirring a pot of pretend tomato sauce might label his play as "playing Daddy" when asked the question, "What are you playing?"

3. **Roles with Rules and Beginning Scenarios.** In this stage, children plan out their roles with their play partners. For example, before playing in the dramatic play area the children decide who will be the waitress, who will be the chef, and who will be the customer. If someone acts out of character, such as a chef taking the customer's order, the child might be chastised by the other children in the group and told, "Noooo, only the waitress can take the order!" The play scenarios in this stage typically last fifteen to twenty minutes.

4. **Mature Roles, Planned Scenarios, and Symbolic Props.** In addition to planning out their roles, children plan out their scenario before they play. Their scenarios are more complex and can be sustained for at least an hour or even over several days. Their roles can change and evolve in response to the play. For example, a group of children decide to run a beauty salon. They decide that one person will cut hair and one person will work the cash register. As the play continues they realize they need someone to wash hair as well, so they create a hair-washing station using a bowl as a prop for the sink.

5. **Dramatization, Multiple Themes, Multiple Roles, and Director's Play.** In this most mature form of make-believe play, children often spend more time planning out their play scenario than actually playing. Children can take on multiple roles during the play, and their scenarios can change in response to who is playing. The play can sustain for several days and even a week or more. For example, a group of children decide they are going to put on a wedding. They create invitations and programs, they gather swatches of fabric to make a wedding dress, and they make instruments for the band. After a week or so of planning they have the actual wedding and reception. Over the next few days, other children join in and decide that they too want to get married, and they act out the wedding again and again.

RECOMMENDED TIME FRAMES FOR CHOICE TIME

Workshop and Recess by Grade Level

Choice Time Workshop

Grade Level	Length of Time	Number of Days per Week
Pre-Kindergarten	45–60 minutes	5
Kindergarten	45 minutes	5
First grade	45 minutes	3–5
Second grade	45 minutes	2–3
Third through fifth grades	45 minutes	1–2

We recommend a forty-five-minute time slot for choice time in order for children to engage in collaborative projects with depth; hence, choice time workshop is typically fewer days a week as children move up through the grades.

Extra Recess

Grade Level	Length of Time	Number of Days per Week
Pre-Kindergarten	30-45 minutes	5
Kindergarten	30 minutes	5
First grade	20–30 minutes	3–5
Second grade	20 minutes	3–5
Third through fifth grades	20 minutes	2–3

We recommend short bursts of extra physical activity multiple times a week in order to give children a brain break from academic tasks. Depending on a teacher's schedule, in the lower grades the thirty-minute time slot is sometimes broken into two fifteen-minute periods for extra recess daily.

APPENDIX C

READING PARTNER GAMES

Possible Games:

- **Play Shared Reading.** Use a Popsicle stick. If it's my book, I point, and we read together.

- **Guided Reading.** I tell the other person what the book is about, and the other person reads it while I help her.

- **On Stage (Broadway Stars).** We read the book together, pick a part, and act it out (use your hands, voice, face, and words to act it out).

- **Echo.** One person reads the page, and then the other person reads the page.

- **American Idol.** We sing the book.

- **Guess My Book.** Partner 1 puts all her books out in front of her and retells one of the books. The other person guesses which book it is. The person has to give their WHOLE retell before she can guess the book.

- **What's Next.** One partner reads a page and guesses what will happen on the next page. It's important that the child who knows the book is asking the other person because it's a new book to her.

- **He Said/She Said.** Have a speech bubble on a Popsicle stick, and readers think what the characters might be saying.

- **Five-Finger Retell.** Read the book together. One partner touches the other partner's fingers to retell it.

- **Guess the Word.** Cover words with a sticky note during independent reading time. One word can be covered, but it has to be a word with a picture, and the partner has to guess what the picture is.

- **Follow the Finger.** One partner points, and the other reads. If the pointer freezes, the reader has to freeze (the reader chooses the book so it's a book he or she knows).

BOOKS FOR CHILDREN ABOUT SOCIAL JUSTICE AND ACTIVISM

A Sweet Smell of Roses by Angela Johnson, illustrated by Eric Velazquez

The air is filled with the smell of roses as two young girls quietly leave their house to witness a civil rights march. This book gives children insights into the concept of organizing for social justice.

Click, Clack, Moo: Cows That Type by Doreen Cronin, Illustrated by Betsy Lewin

In Click, Clack, Moo, the cows and hens are farm workers negotiating for better conditions. They are cold at night and ask for electric blankets. When the farmer refuses, they form a coalition with the hens who are also cold. They threaten to strike if their demand isn't met. With a duck as negotiator, they get their blankets. This is a funny story about the power of collaboration and negotiation.

Hey Little Ant! by Philip and Hannah Hoose, illustrated by Debbie Tilley

This story is a debate between an ant and a little boy who is about to squish it. The story can lead to powerful discussions that children can relate to about the use and abuse of power.

How to Heal a Broken Wing by Bob Graham

Everyone walks by an injured pigeon on a busy Manhattan street–everyone but Will. Will puts the pigeon in a box and takes it home to nurse it back to health and ultimately releases it. It's a beautiful tale about caring for the most vulnerable among us.

The Peace Book by Todd Parr

This book gives kids accessible messages about peace that include: Peace is giving new shoes to someone who needs them. Peace is making new friends. Peace is having enough pizza in the world for everyone.

The Streets Are Free by Kurusa, illustrated by Monika Doppert

This book, based on a true story, is about children living in in a crowded neighborhood in Caracas, Venezuela. They have no place to play, and when they try to play in the street, they are chased away. The children mobilize the community to take action and they confront the politicians at city hall.

Swimmy by Leo Lionni

This is a story about Swimmy, a fish swimming alone and constantly in fear of being eaten by a bigger fish. When he finds a school of fish that are hiding because they're also afraid of being eaten, Swimmy organizes them to swim together in the shape of a giant fish. This is a story about the power of working together as a community that will resonate with our youngest children.

APPENDIX E

STUDENT INTEREST RECORDING SHEET

Observing Student Interests

Week of: _____

| *Drawing Topics | *Writing Topics | *Book Choices | *Play Themes |
| *Play Area Choices | *Material Choices | *Seating Choices | *Conversations with Peers |

Name:	Name:	Name:	Name:
Name:	Name:	Name:	Name:
Name:	Name:	Name:	Name:
Name:	Name:	Name:	Name:
Name:	Name:	Name:	Name:

APPENDIX F

QUESTIONS TO HELP YOU LEARN MORE ABOUT YOUR STUDENTS

Questions to Consider When Observing for Children's Interests

- When given free time to draw, what topics does the child draw?
- When given free choice to write, what topics does the child write about?
- When given free range of the library, what books does the child settle with?
- What are the child's most common play themes in free play?
- What does the child talk about with her peers at unstructured times?
- When given free choice, what is a child most drawn to: running around, talking with friends, or drawing?
- What tasks does the child seem most engaged in? Least engaged in?
- Does the child prefer large groups? Small? To be on his own?
- What part of the room is the child most drawn to? The rug? The tables?
- What materials is the child most drawn to? What about during recess?

Questions to Ask When Talking with Children

It can be helpful to give children ample time to answer or draw their responses. You may even ask follow-up questions that help you understand more deeply, things like: why, say more, or anything else?

- What do you like to do when you have free time?
- Where is your favorite place to work?
- Who are your favorite people to work with?
- Do you prefer to work on your own or with others?
- How loud or quiet do you like it when you work?
- What do you wish our classroom had?
- What do you wish our recess area had?
- If you could design the classroom, what would you change?
- What things do you like to read about? Watch on TV? Learn about from the Internet?
- Who is your hero? Can you say why?

OUR FAVORITE BOOKS ABOUT THE TEACHING OF READING

The Art of Teaching Reading by Lucy Calkins

Becoming Literate by Marie Clay

Growing Readers by Kathy Collins

Conferring with Readers by Gravity Goldberg and Jennifer Serravallo

Guided Reading by Irene Fountas and Gay Su Pinnell

I Am Reading: Nurturing Young Children's Meaning Making and Joyful Engagement by Kathy Collins and Matt Glover

Teaching Reading in Small Groups by Jennifer Serravallo

The Reading Strategies Book by Jennifer Serravallo

BIBLIOGRAPHY

Blackburn, Barbara R. 2013. *Rigor Is Not a Four-Letter Word* (2nd Ed.). New York: Routledge.

Bodrova, Elena and Deborah Leong. 2007. *Tools of the Mind: The Vygotskian Approach to Early Childhood Education.* Upper Saddle River, NJ: Pearson Education.

_____. 2012. "Assessing and Scaffolding Make Believe Play." *Young Children.* Washington, DC: National Association for the Education of Young Children.

_____. Spring 2015. *American Journal of Play* 7(3), 371.

Brown, Stuart L., with Christopher C. Vaughan. 2010. *Play: How It Shapes the Brain, Opens the Imagination, and Invigorates the Soul.* New York: Avery.

Bruner, Jerome. 1978. *The Selected Works of Jerome S. Bruner.* New York: Routledge.

Cambourne, Brian. 1993. *The Whole Story: Natural Learning and the Acquisition of Literacy in the Classroom.* New York: Scholastic.

Carlson, Frances. 2011. *Big Body Play: Why Boisterous, Vigorous, and Very Physical Play Is Essential to Children's Development and Learning.* Washington, DC: National Association for the Education of Young Children.

Charney, Ruth Sidney. 2002. *Teaching Children to Care.* Northeast Foundation for Children.

Clay, Marie. 1993. *An Observation Survey of Early Literacy Achievement.* Portsmouth, NH: Heinemann.

Costa, Arthur L. and Bena Kallick. 2014. *Dispositions: Reframing Teaching and Learning.* Thousand Oaks, CA: Corwin.

Cowley, Joy. 2015. "The Power of Story." *Journal of Reading Recovery* 14(2), Worthington, OH: Reading Recovery Council of North America.

Cuffaro, H. K. 1995. *Experimenting with the World: John Dewey and the Early Childhood Classroom.* New York: Teachers College Press.

Drew, Walter F., James Christie, James E. Johnson, Alice M. Meckley, and Marcia L. Nell. 2008. "Constructive Play: A Value-Added Strategy for Meeting Early Learning Standards." *Young Children* (38–44). Washington, DC: National Association for the Education of Young Children.

Dweck, Carol S. 2006. *Mindset: The New Psychology of Success*. New York: Ballantine Books.

———. 2013. *The Power of Yet*. YouTube. Jan. 26, 2013.

Edwards, Carolyn, Lella Gandini, and George Forman, Eds. 1998. *The Hundred Languages of Children: The Reggio Emilia Approach—Advanced Reflections*. Westport, CT: Ablex.

Elkind, David. 2007. *The Power of Play: Learning What Comes Naturally*. Philadelphia: Da Capo Press.

Feynman, Richard and Ralph Leighton. 1997. *Surely You're Joking Mr. Feynman! (Adventures of a Curious Character)*. New York: W. W. Norton & Company.

Gardner, Howard. 1993. *Multiple Intelligences: New Horizons in Theory and Practice*. New York: Perseus.

Gandini, L. 1998. "Education and Caring Spaces" in Edwards, C., Gandini, L., & Forman, G. *The Hundred Languages of Children*. Greenwich, CT: Ablex.

Goleman, Daniel P. 2005. *Emotional Intelligence: Why It Can Matter More Than IQ*. New York: Bantam Books.

Graves, Donald H. 1985. *Writing: Teachers and Children at Work*. Portsmouth, NH: Heinemann.

Gray, Peter. 2013. *Free to Learn*. New York: Basic Books.

Hatch, Thomas. 1990. "Social Intelligence in Young Children." Paper delivered at the annual meeting of the American Psychological Association.

Hattie, John and Gregory C. R. Yates. 2014. *Visible Learning and the Science of How We Learn*. New York: Routledge.

Heard, Georgia and Jennifer McDonough. 2009. *A Place for Wonder: Reading and Writing Nonfiction in the Primary Grades*. Portland, ME: Stenhouse Publishers.

Johnston, Peter H. 1997. *Knowing Literacy: Constructive Literacy Assessment*. Portland, ME: Stenhouse Publishers.

Kohn, Alfie. 1993. *Punished by Rewards*. New York: Houghton Mifflin.

Koste, V. Glasgow. 1995. *Dramatic Play in Childhood: Rehearsal for Life*. Portsmouth, NH: Heinemann.

Krechevsky, Mara, Ben Mardell, Melissa Rivard, and Daniel Wilson. 2013. *Visible Learners: Promoting Reggio-Inspired Approaches in All Schools*. San Francisco, CA: Jossey-Bass.

Krock, Lexi. 2011. "Accidental Discoveries" *Researchhistory.org*

Kurusa. 2008. *The Streets Are Free*. Toronto: Annick Press.

Leana, Carrie R. 2011. "The Missing Link in School Reform." *Stanford Social Innovation Review*, 9(4): 30–35. Stanford, CA: Stanford University.

Lester, Stuart L. and Wendy Russell. 2008. *Play for a Change: Play, Policy, and Practice: A Review of Contemporary Perspectives*. London: Play England.

Levin, Diane E. May 2003. "Beyond Banning War and Superhero Play: Meeting Children's Needs in Violent Times." *Young Children*. Washington, DC: National Association for the Education of Young Children.

Lindfors, Judith Wells. 1999. *Children's Inquiry: Using Language to Make Sense of the World*. New York: Teachers College Press.

Martinelli, Marjorie and Kristine Mraz. 2012. *Smarter Charts: Optimizing an Instructional Staple to Create Independent Readers and Writers*. Portsmouth, NH: Heinemann.

Marzano, Robert and Debra Pickering. 2011. *Classroom Instruction That Works*. Alexandria, Virginia: Association for Supervision and Curriculum Development.

Mraz, Kristine and Marjorie Martinelli. 2014. *Smarter Charts for Math, Science, and Social Studies: Making Learning Visible in the Content Areas*. Portsmouth, NH: Heinemann.

Mraz, Kristine and Christine Hertz. 2015. *A Mindset for Learning: Teaching the Traits of Mindful, Joyful Independent Growth*. Portsmouth, NH: Heinemann.

National Council for Social Studies. 2013. *College, Career, and Civic Life Framework for Social Studies State Standards*. Silver Spring, MD: NCSS.

National Science Teachers Association. 2004. Position Statement on Scientific Inquiry. www.nsta.org/about/positions/inquiry.

National Governors Association for Best Practices (NGA Center) and Council of Chief State School Officers (CCSSO). 2010. *Common Core State Standards for English Language Arts and Literacy in History/Social Studies, Science, and Technical Subjects.* Washington, DC: NGA Center and CCSSO.

Noddings, Nell. 2004. *Happiness and Education.* New York: Cambridge University Press.

_____. 2013. *Caring: A Relational Approach to Ethics and Moral Education (Updated Edition).* Oakland, CA: University of California Press.

_____. 1991. Stories in dialogue: Caring and interpersonal reasoning. In C. Wityherell and N. Noddings (Eds.), *Stories lives tell: Narrative and dialogue in education.* New York: Teachers College Press, 157–170.

Paley, Vivian Gussin. 2005. *A Child's Work: The Importance of Fantasy Play.* Chicago: University of Chicago Press.

_____. 1986. *Mollie Is Three: Growing Up in School.* Chicago: University of Chicago Press.

Parten, Mildred B. 1932. "Stages of Imaginary Play: Social Participation Among Pre-School Children." *The Journal of Abnormal and Social Psychology*, Vol. 27(3), Oct 1932, 243–269. Minneapolis, MN: University of Minnesota.

Pellegrini, Anthony. Fall 2008. "The Recess Debate." *American Journal of Play* 1(2).

Perry, Bruce D., and Maia Szalavitz. 2011. *Born for Love: Why Empathy Is Essential—and Endangered.* New York: William Morrow Paperbacks.

Peterson, Bob. 2007. "Teaching for Social Justice: One Teacher's Journey." In *Rethinking Our Classrooms: Teaching for Equity and Justice, Volume 1.* Milwaukee, WI: Rethinking Schools Limited.

Porcelli, Allison, and Cheryl Tyler. 2008. *A Quick Guide to Boosting English Acquisition in Choice Time.* Portsmouth, NH: Heinemann.

Raschka, Chris. 2013. *Everyone Can Learn to Ride a Bicycle.* New York: Schwartz & Wade.

Ray, Katie Wood. January 2006. "Exploring an Inquiry Stance in the Writing Workshop." *Language Arts* 83(3). Urbana, IL: National Council of Teachers of English.

Schwartz, Shanna. 2008. *A Quick Guide to Making Your Teaching Stick.* Portsmouth, NH: Heinemann.

Serravallo, Jennifer. 2010. *Teaching Reading in Small Groups.* Portsmouth, NH: Heinemann.

Short, Kathy G., Jerome C. Harste, and Carolyn Burke. 1996. *Creating Classrooms for Authors and Inquirers (2nd Ed).* Portsmouth, NH: Heinemann.

Sicart, Miguel. 2014. *Play Matters.* Cambridge, MA: The MIT Press.

Thiel, Jaye Johnson. 2014. "Privileged Play: The Risky Business of Language in the Primary Classroom" *Perspectives and Provocations* 4(1). Early Childhood Education Assembly, NCTE.

Vygotsky, Lev S. 1978. *Mind in Society: The Development of Higher Psychological Processes.* Cambridge, MA: Harvard University Press.

_____. 1966. "Play and Its Role in the Mental Development of the Child." *Voprosy Psikhologii* 6. Online version published by Psychology and Marxism Internet Archive (marxists.org) 2002.

Wagner, Tony. 2008. *The Global Achievement Gap.* New York: Basic Books.

Weisberg, D. S., J. M. Zosh, K. Hirsh-Pasek, and R. M. Golinkoff. 2013. "Talking It Up: Play, Language Development and the Role of Adult Support." *American Journal of Play* 6(1), Rochester, NY: The Strong National Museum of Play.

Weintraub, Pamela. June 2015. "The Voice of Reason." *Psychology Today.* New York: Sussex Publishers.

Whitin, Phyllis, and David Whitin. 1997. *Inquiry at the Window: Pursuing the Wonders of Learners.* Portsmouth, NH: Heinemann.